RAILWAY BYLINES
SUMMER SPECIAL No.5

Isle of Wight O2 No.28 ASHEY approaches Ryde St.Johns Road with a Cowes train on 26 August 1964.
PHOTOGRAPH: PETER GROOM

CONTENTS

4   **The Tweed Valley Line**
Tweedmouth-Kelso-St.Boswells

26   **Further fine photos**
Industrial pictures by *W.J.Ford*

30   **A flurry of forecourts**
Station forecourts

32   **A contractor's job**
A contractor's railway – 1950s style

36   **Barrington Cement Works**
by *Ian Peaty*

52   **Both sides of the Dart**
Kingswear and Dartmouth

56   **Fourum**
Far Tottering & Oyster Creek Railway

58   **Cross Hands and Tumble**
Not a dance but a Welsh railtour

72   **Es on the Island**
E1 0-6-0Ts on the Isle of Wight

74   **The Cuckoo Line**
Railwayman's reminiscences

80   **Transporter of Delights**
Photographs by *Douglas Robinson*

84   **Grand Canal Street shed**
An Irish shed, by *Desmond Coakham*

96   **And finally…**
Unusual Manx wildlife

Editor
Martin Smith

All correspondence regarding editorial matters should be addressed to;
RAILWAY BYLINES
P.O.BOX 1957, RADSTOCK, BATH BA3 5YJ
Tel: 01373-812048
(office hours only please)
Fax: 01373-0813610
E-mail: smudger@ivycot49.freeserve.co.uk

Views expressed by contributors are not necessarily those of the editor or publisher. Information is published in good faith, but no liability can be accepted for loss or inconvenience arising from error or omission.
The editor will be pleased to consider contributions (articles, photographs or whatever) for publication but, while every reasonable care will be taken, no responsibility can be accepted for loss or damage, howsoever caused.
In the case of manuscripts submitted for publication, the editor reserves the right to amend the text, if necessary, to suit the style of the magazine. Where possible, edited/amended texts will be returned to the contributor for his/her approval, but the final decision rests with the editor.

The magazine RAILWAY BYLINES is published monthly by Irwell Press Ltd., 59a High Street, Clophill, Beds MK45 4BE. It is printed in Luton by JetSpeed and distributed by COMAG, London.
All distribution enquiries regarding the NEWSTRADE and MODEL SHOPS should be directed to Magazine Subscriptions, PO Box 464, Berkhamsted, Herts HP4 2UR.
COPYRIGHT IRWELL PRESS 2002
ALL RIGHTS RESERVED

Main cover photo. One of the Isle of Man's famous Beyer Peacock 2-4-0Ts pulls into Castletown in July 1964. PHOTOGRAPH: DOUGLAS ROBINSON

Upper cover photo. Narrow gauge at Wellingborough Quarries – Stewarts & Lloyds's Peckett 0-6-0ST No.85 climbs away from the quarries on the metre gauge system on 2 June 1966. PHOTOGRAPH: PETER GROOM

Top right. The view from the footbridge – 5649 prepares to pull away from Aberavon Town on 1 July 1961. PHOTOGRAPH: ALEC SWAIN; THE TRANSPORT TREASURY

Bottom right. Industrials R Us… Andrew Barclay 0-4-0ST WELLINGTON in the exchange sidings at Ellistown Colliery, about ten miles to the north-west of Leicester, on 29 April 1963. PHOTOGRAPH: R.C.RILEY THE TRANSPORT TREASURY

Right. Off for a ramble? The gentleman at Llangammarch Wells on 2 October 1971 looks reasonably prepared. PHOTOGRAPH: ANDREW MUCKLEY

Rear cover photo. Kingswear station and harbour, 20 June 1957. There's more inside! PHOTOGRAPH: JOHN R.BONSER

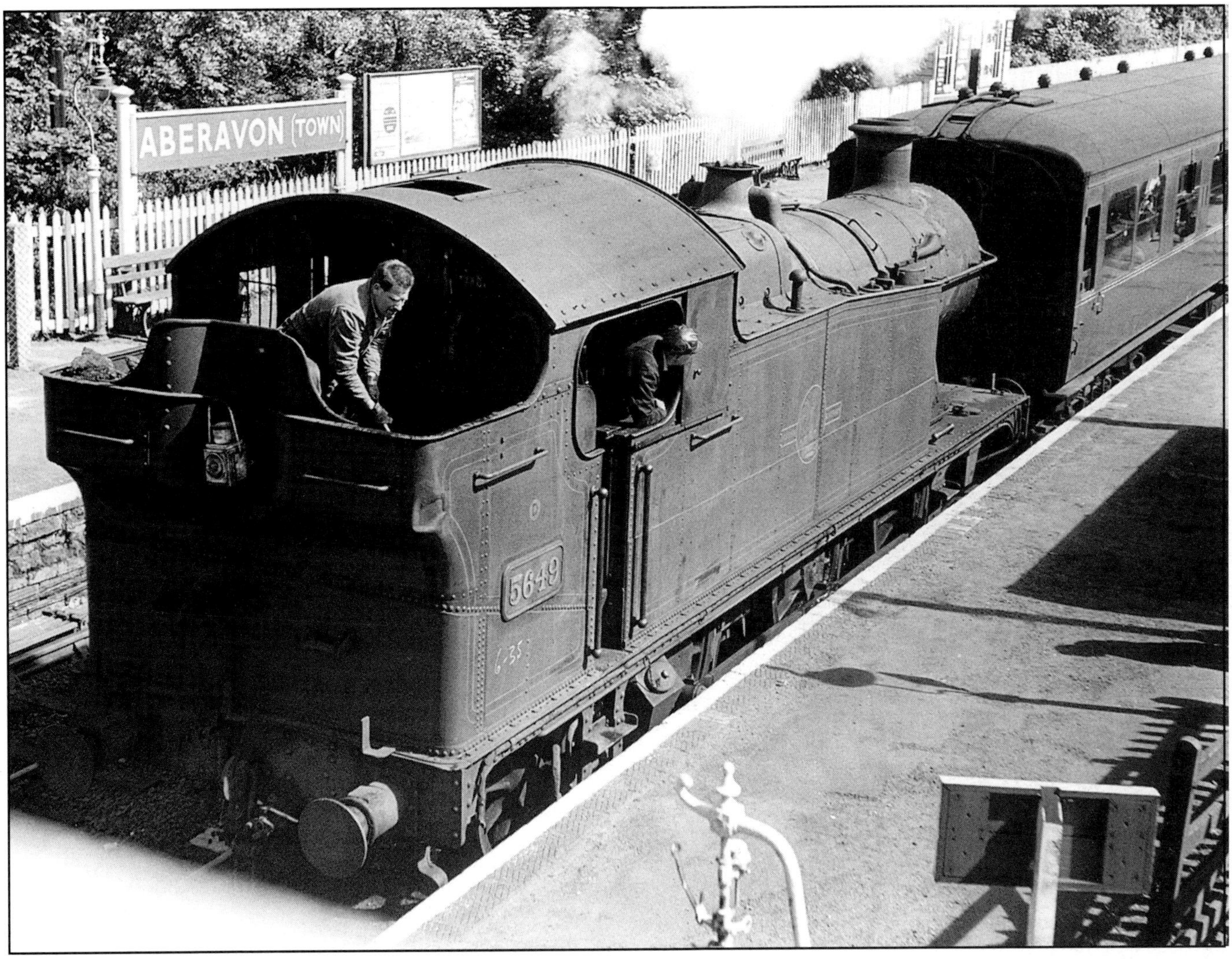
ABERAVON (TOWN)
5649

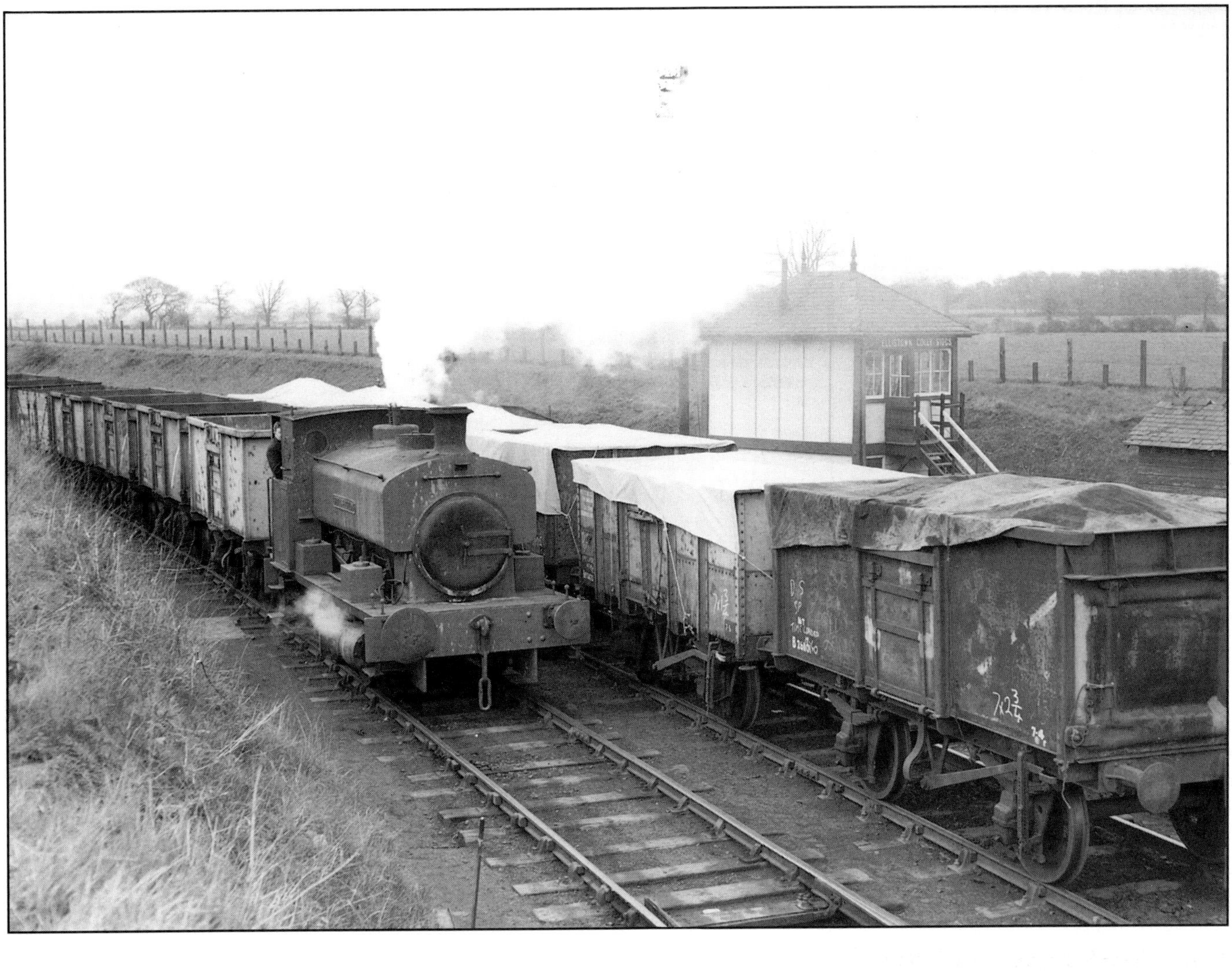

THE TWEED VALLEY LINE
Tweedmouth to St.Boswells

by A.J.Mullay and I.C.Coleford

The western end of the Tweed Valley line – for passenger trains, at least – was St.Boswells station. On 12 June 1954 G5 0-4-4T No.67268 (just ten months away from withdrawal) waits in the bay at the south end of the station with the 7.15pm to Tweedmouth and Berwick. On shed are J36 No.65331 (with tender cab) and an unidentified J35. PHOTOGRAPH: W.A.C.SMITH

The River Tweed drains around 1,870 square miles and reaches the North Sea at Berwick, the last stretch of its 97 winding miles comprising a broad valley from St.Boswells eastwards, with Kelso the largest town. The Tweed Valley line ran westwards from Tweedmouth on the East Coast Main Line, parallelled the river and crossed the Anglo-Scottish border near Carham, and ended almost 34 miles away at St.Boswells on the Waverley Route. A tourist stumbling on the line in the early 1960s could be forgiven for imagining that they had discovered a typically sleepy branch line. Yet this was once an important cross-Border railway which figured large in the minds of opposing rail company promoters and, from an operational point of view, provided a rare example of a railway changing ownership in the middle of a signalling section.

Although the railway was widely known, particularly among railway enthusiasts, as the Tweed Valley line and although it was the only public railway wholly within the valley of the Tweed, that title was never used by the railway companies. It was a generic term for what were actually *two* branches – one from the east and one from the west – which met end-on near Kelso. The line from the east was constructed by the York, Newcastle & Berwick Railway and that from the west by the North British Railway, and both companies called their lines 'the Kelso branch'.

But whether referred to by its official or its unofficial title, the line never lived up to the aspirations the shareholders once held for it. It did, however, provide a diversionary route for Britain's most important expresses on a number of occasions, and its metals carried the non-stop *Flying Scotsman* and the *Queen of Scots* Pullman. More of this anon...

A broad view of the mid-19th century history of railway construction across the Border would seem to indicate that railway companies from each country were generally prepared to construct as far as the Border, or nearby town, and then connect with a company coming in the opposite direction. Superficially, it might have seemed that 'collaborating' companies enjoyed good relations, but there was invariably an element of suspicion – neither could rule out the

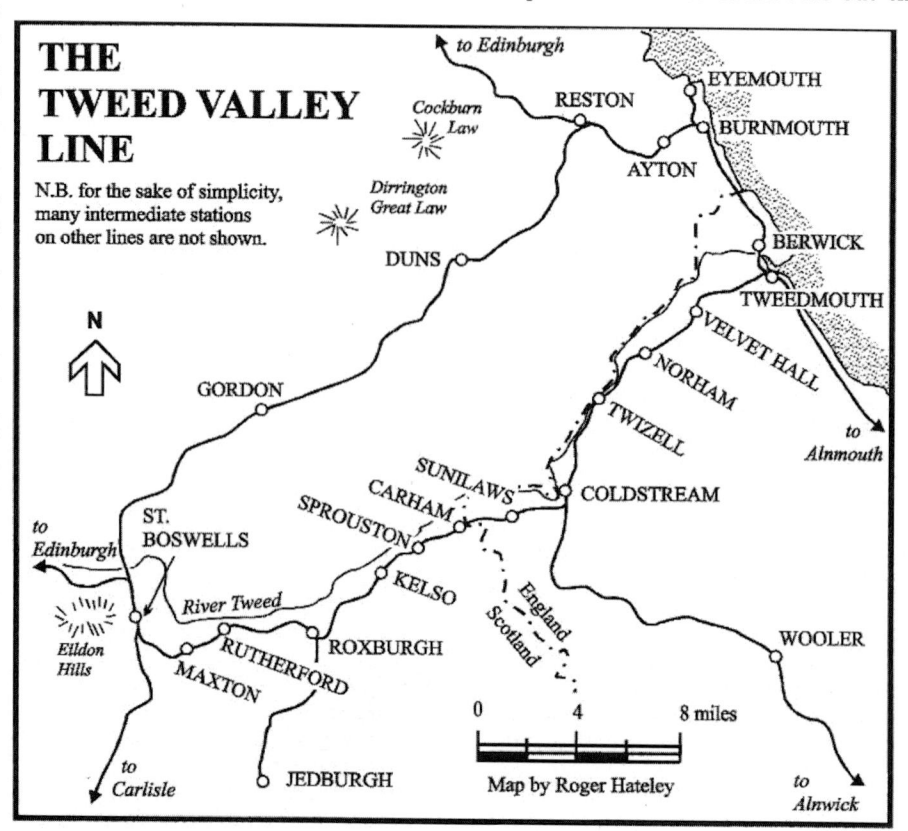

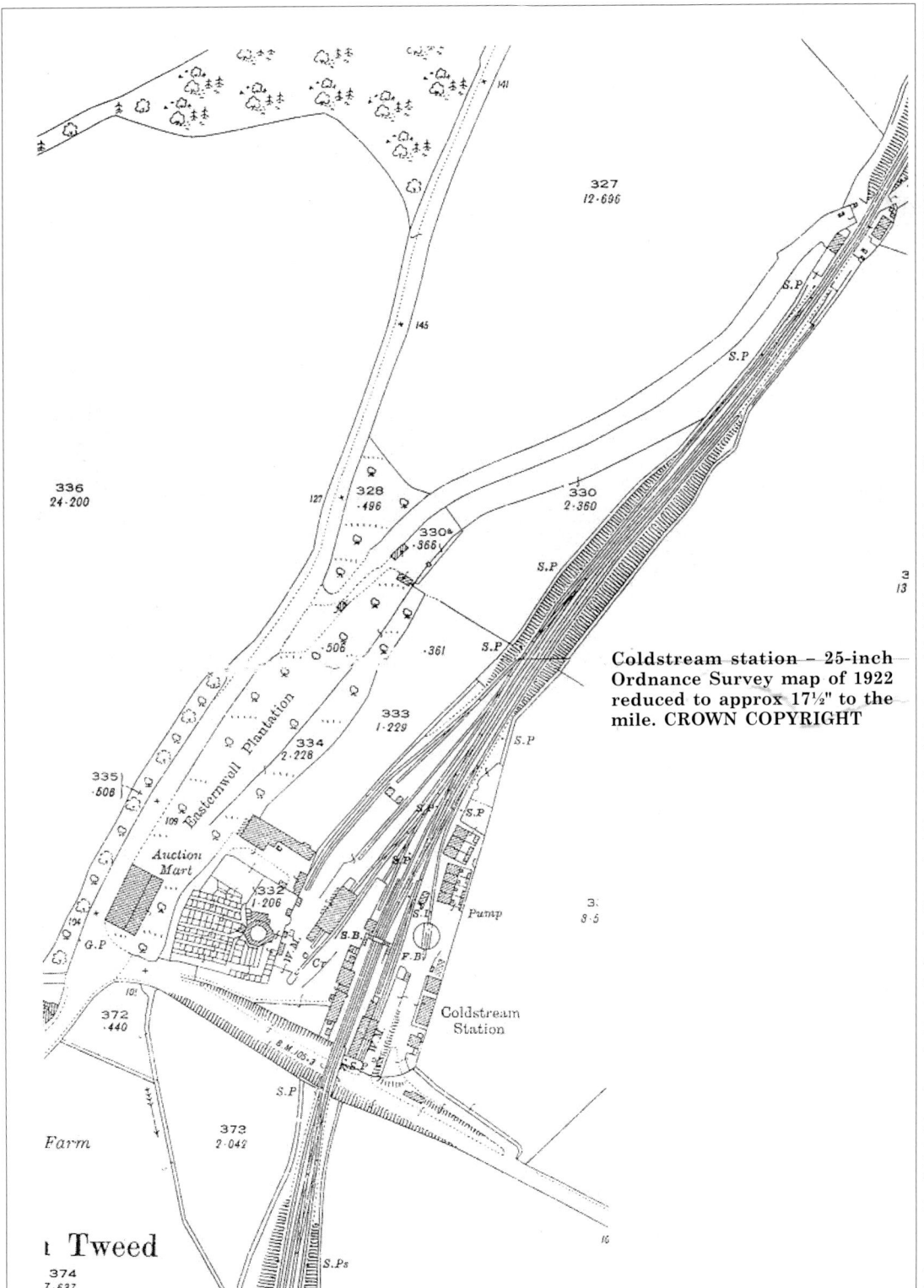

Coldstream station – 25-inch Ordnance Survey map of 1922 reduced to approx 17½" to the mile. CROWN COPYRIGHT

COLDSTREAM (Berwick)
Miles 349. Map Sq. 3.
Pop. 1,294. Clos. day Thur.
From King's Cross via Berwick.
1st cl.—Single 81/8, Return 163/4.
3rd cl.—Single 54/5, Return 108/10.

Kg's X a.m.	Cold. a.m.	Cold. a.m.	Kg's X p.m.
12 55r	10 27	9 9r	6 12
p.m.	p.m.	p.m.	a.m.
10 10r	7 15	5 4	3 3

No Sunday Trains.
e Not Saturday.
r Refreshment Car.
s Saturday only.

From the *ABC Railway Guide*, 1956

by opportunistic businessmen who intended more than a link between Edinburgh and Berwick. Any approach towards the lucrative English markets was of interest to them.

Miller does not appear to have taken his instructions too literally and his plans for a Tweed Valley line ran eastwards from St.Boswells only as far as Sprouston, just east of Kelso. This was because the English were moving even faster. The Newcastle & Berwick Railway (which was to become a component of the York, Newcastle & Berwick Railway [YN&B] in August 1847) was busily constructing a branch line westwards along the valley of the Tweed, and any thought that this might be exclusively intended to cater for local traffic was dispelled by a newspaper report in 1848 which opined that the 'North Eastern lobby' (*sic*) could view a Tweed Valley line as a launch-pad for a main line to Edinburgh independent of the NBR. This may have been intended as a Stock Exchange attack to depress NBR shares when George Hudson, the York-based 'Railway King' was active in the market, but it illustrates the highly suspicious nature of relations between the NBR and the YN&B, despite the fact that those two companies became allies on the soon-to-be-completed East Coast Main Line.

The YN&B opens
The YN&B's line between Berwick and Sprouston was virtually complete by late July 1849 and was subjected to the obligatory Board of Trade inspection on the 23rd of that month. The inspecting officer, Captain Wynne, reported that the line '...extends to a temporary terminus within two miles of the town of Kelso'. Captain Wynne noted that, as the 133-yard-long 89-feet-high stone viaduct over the River Till, near Twizell, was not quite finished, a single line was carried over

possibility that the other would attempt to penetrate their territory by building a line through the central Borders to reach either Edinburgh or Newcastle.

The Tweed Valley line was the product of this mutual suspicion, with the Scottish and English sections of the railway being planned and constructed, not in harmony, nor for the benefit of the travelling public, but to block each other. This explains the end-on junction in the middle of a section, which might have been more appropriately situated at one of the principal intermediate stations such as Kelso or Coldstream. Farther north in Berwickshire, such a junction was constructed at Duns where the privately-floated Berwickshire Railway made a connection with the NBR branch from Reston (*see the Railway Bylines Annual No.4.*), but the Tweed Valley line was so different in so many ways.

Origins
A waggonway between Berwick and Kelso had been authorised by Act of Parliament in 1811, but it was never constructed. Revised plans of 1824 suffered a similar fate and were formally abandoned in 1838. Another proposal came in 1844 when the fledgling North British Railway, which was just beginning to construct its main line from Edinburgh to Berwick-upon-Tweed, instructed its engineer, John Miller, to survey a route 'to the south... and to consider taking the Berwick and Kelso line as a branch'. This was an early indication that the NBR was being driven

A little over 5½ miles along the line from Tweedmouth was Norham. We are looking east towards the station on 14 April 1963. The modest goods facilities can be seen on the down side of the line – the goods shed was originally an engine shed. The station is now in private ownership, albeit without track. PHOTOGRAPH: W.A.C.SMITH

the river on a temporary viaduct; he advised that '...as a measure of precaution all trains should pass very slowly over the timber bridge'. He noted that '...the platforms, though not quite finished, are sufficiently advanced to render ingress and egress to and from the carriages safe and easy'. Being generally satisfied with the works, Captain Wynne recommended that the line could be opened to public passenger traffic. This it did the following Friday, 27 July 1849.

Not mentioned in the BoT report were three other viaducts spanning tributaries of the Tweed: at Newbiggen Dene (6 arches, 134 yards long and no less than 103 feet high), East Learmouth (5 arches, 94 yards long, 60 fet high) and West Learmouth (7 arches, 118 yards long, 62 feet high).

All the stations on the Tweedmouth-Kelso line had loading banks to deal with agricultural traffic. That such traffic was almost exclusively anticipated is confirmed by NER historian, J.C.Dean, in the *North Eastern Express* (the journal of the North Eastern Railway Association): 'The company seems to have made a point of avoiding such few villages as there were along the line. Velvet Hall – so called after an adjacent farm – was over a mile from the nearest village, Horncliffe. Norham village was a good half-mile from the station and, as far as I can see, Twizell merely served a couple of farms...'.

In the run-up to, and in the aftermath of, the opening of the line, the YN&B's directors and management had to deal with all manner of routine matters. The following are just a few random extracts from the company minute books:

30 May 1849: 'Mr.Harrison *(Thomas Harrison, a director of the YN&B – later the NER's chief engineer)* be authorised to make such arrangements as he thinks fit for building stables at Cornhill and Sprouston which are represented to be absolutely necessary'.

28 June 1849: 'Mr.Allport *(later Sir James of Midland Railway fame)* be authorised to place such efficient servants at the Stations on the Kelso Branch as can be removed from the Main Line'.

15 September 1849: '...the Directors desire no steps to be taken in relation to the Temporary Goods Warehouses at Sprouston, or the Stable there, or Lime or Goods Depots at Norham and Cornhill, until further orders be given by them...'

10 November 1849: '...a goods warehouse be erected at Sprouston from part of the materials of Newcastle Old Station'.

25 January 1850: '...To decline allowing any private agents at the stations... and Mr.Harrison be instructed to get the Lime Sheds on the Kelso branch properly covered... and Mr.Markie to report as to any improvement which might be made to prevent breakage of the coals'

8 February 1850: '...proposed...that the porter at the Sprouston station who was found to be guilty of stealing corn belonging to the horses be discharged. A saving of a porter will be effected at this station which will amount to £40 per annum'.

19 September 1851: 'Resolved that ...the evening train on the Kelso Branch be discontinued from the 1st of October"

13 August 1852: '...the [goods] shed at Sprouston be removed to Cornhill'.

Such were the everyday requirements of running a railway.

The Tweedmouth-Sprouston line threw up a few idiosyncrasies. One was that Coldstream's station was situated at Cornhill, south of the Tweed – i.e. in a different *country* to the town it nominally served! Another was that Sprouston and Carham stations were two of only three railway stations built in Scotland by a pre-grouping English company. (For the record, the third was Annan Shawhill on the Solway Junction Railway – although the SJR was worked by the Caledonian, it was an English company.)

Coming from Scotland

The YN&B might have opened its line in 1849, but the NBR, having been slowed by appallingly expensive land purchases on both its Hawick and Kelso branches, lagged behind. It finally opened its line from St.Boswells, but only as far as a temporary station at Wallacenick, almost a mile short of Kelso, on 17 June 1850. This station was described by the Board of Trade as '...being in a deep cutting and most inconveniently circumstanced both for the passenger and goods traffic'. It was not until 27 January 1851 that the line was extended by 75 chains* to the permanent station at Kelso. That said, the station was actually in Maxwellheugh, on the opposite side of the Tweed to the town itself and up a fairly steep hill. *(*80 chains = 1 mile.)*

The final link in the chain was the 2¼-mile section between Kelso and Sprouston. The eastern half of this 'missing link' was built by the YN&B and the western half by the NBR. The two sections met end-on at 'Sprouston Junction' which was, in fact, at Mellendean Burn, a mile west of Sprouston.

The opening of this 'missing link' on 1 June 1851 completed the through line between Tweedmouth and St.Boswells.

As for the end-on junction at 'Sprouston', most unusually it was in the middle of the countryside. In later years

Twizell station, looking towards Tweedmouth, 26 April 1952. The facilities are, shall we say, unassuming. The small goods yard – little more than a loading dock and a siding – are beyond the platform on the right. The timber signal box is on a brick base. If the date of this picture were 1962, not 1952, we would be tempted to suggest that the member of staff crossing the line has been watching too many Chuck Berry performances. PHOTOGRAPH: J.W.ARMSTRONG TRUST

Coldstream station, looking west. So far was Coldstream station from the town it served, that it was more honest to call it 'Cornhill' as the constructing company did until 1873. It was actually situated in the Northumberland village of that name. When Professor Balfour brought his plant-pickers here in 1857 (see text), they had to walk across to Scotland to find beds for the night, before botanising along the Tweed next day and returning to England to catch a train at Norham. But what of the scene here? An inspection trolley (a Wickham 17A?) is parked on the siding immediately behind the rear of the down platform, while a coal wagon stands near the coal drops on the siding on the extreme left. PHOTOGRAPH: PAUL CHANCELLOR COLLECTION

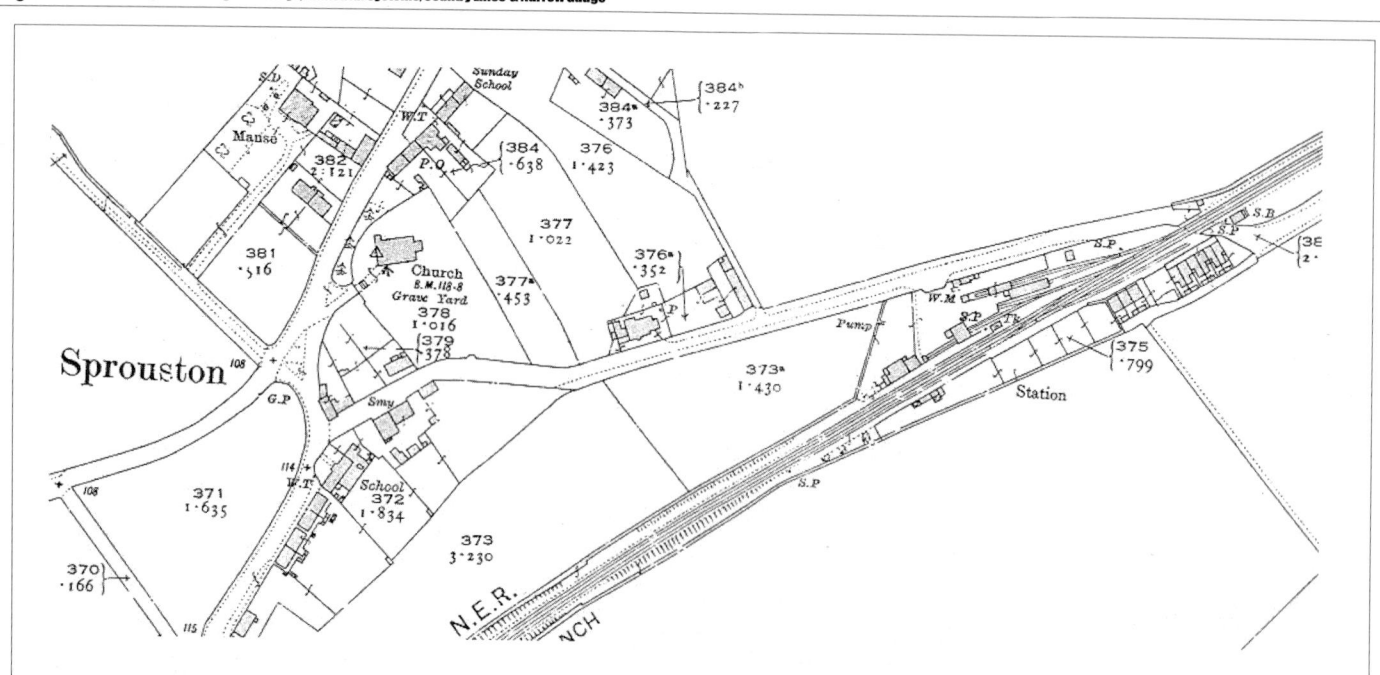

Sprouston station – 25-inch Ordnance Survey map of 1921 reduced to approx 17½" to the mile. Note the engine shed crammed in between two goods sidings at the east end of the station. CROWN COPYRIGHT

it was claimed that the only indicator of a change of line ownership at the 'junction' itself was a difference in the colour of the ballast! It was almost a dress-rehearsal for the meeting of the trans-USA railroad at Promontory Bluffs. The imagination struggles to think of another place in the UK where a line changed ownership without any obvious indication.

Like the YN&B line between Tweedmouth and Sprouston Junction, the entire NBR line between St.Boswells and Sprouston Junction was also double track. However, the NBR section was later singled, as we shall eventually see.

Despite the lowly status of the NBR line, it had cost the company dear. The NBR's arrival in the lower Tweed Valley had triggered the opposition of the Duke of Roxburgh who had refused to allow rail access to his land in the vicinity of Floors Castle north of the river, although his name occured frequently enough in the list of owners who would have to be satisfied by the rail company, so he was certainly prepared to take the railway's gold. Sir George Douglas, who lived nearby, took no less than £25,000 of it, and was 'congratulated' by the railway stockholders' press as having secured the best ever transaction with a railway company at that time. The line was so expensive to build that, when the NBR was planning its line between St.Boswells and Duns fifteen years later, the company treated Berwickshire landowners with great caution and encouraged them to promote their own line.

Sprouston station, looking towards Tweedmouth, 26 April 1952. The station had two water columns fed from the 6,800-gallon tank which can be seen at the end of the platform. PHOTOGRAPH: J.W.ARMSTRONG TRUST

Sprouston engine shed closed in 1916, so it didn't remain in use long enough to attract the attention of Fl/Lt Aidan Fuller (he of 'walk along a cinder path' fame), but as is clearly evident in this picture of 26 April 1952 the structure was still standing and in fairly good condition. It was, however, demolished in the 1960s. Whereas the goods facilities at most of the Tweed Valley stations were fairly spacious, those at Sprouston were rather cramped. The seemingly obligatory coal drops were squeezed in on the siding alongside the engine shed. Note the attractive ground signal. PHOTOGRAPH: J.W.ARMSTRONG TRUST

If nothing else, the fact that the Tweed Valley line did not cross the Tweed even once helped to save money on what was already a very expensive railway to construct. Indeed, to a traveller on the line there was little impression of travelling along a river valley, as the Tweed basin (known locally as the Merse) is so wide as to resemble a plain. An impressive viaduct made a riverine crossing at Roxburgh Junction, but that was over the Teviot.

Along the line

Taking the route as a whole, it nominally started at **Tweedmouth**. That said, by the 1900s most of the branch trains ran through to/from Berwick even though this involved a reversal at Tweedmouth. The procedure for Tweed Valley trains starting at Berwick was for them to run right through Tweedmouth station to a point almost opposite Tweedmouth engine shed; the engine would then propel the train across to the down platform where it would run round in readiness for taking the branch. (Trains arriving from St.Boswells and continuing to Berwick could run directly into the down platform at Tweedmouth; there the engine would run round.)

From Tweedmouth the double-track Tweed Valley line ran on a gentle downward gradient (none of the gradients on the entire Tweedmouth-Kelso line exceeded 1 in 150) across the rich farming land on the south side of the Tweed, then climbed gently to the first station before entering the first station, **Velvet Hall** (4m 10ch from Tweedmouth). It was a typical North Eastern country station with dressed stone buildings on the down platform and a wooden shelter on the up*. That said, writing in the *North Eastern Express*, J.C.Dean opined that the overall impression of Velvet Hall when seen from platform level was '...somewhat spoiled by a hotch-potch of stone and wooden buildings, reflecting development over a period'. There was a signal box at Velvet Hall; it had a 14-lever frame installed in 1880 and a new 15-lever frame in March 1929. (*On the NER section, Down was towards Kelso, Up towards Tweedmouth.)

On leaving Velvet Hall the line gently undulated on its way to **Norham** (6m 53ch), a simple station with a modest goods yard and a signal box. The original timber-built 'box was replaced in 1902 by a brick-built one with a 20-lever frame. Outward goods included milk churns, eggs, salmon, rabbits, game birds, potatoes, sugar beet and grain; goods inwards included household coal, livestock, farm machinery and animal feed. Two Clydesdale horses were kept at the station for local deliveries. The goods shed was originally an engine shed (this explains the most unusual 'twin road' construction) which had been built by the YN&B to house an engine for shunting the goods yards at the eastern end of the Tweed Valley line. For conversion to a goods shed, one road was blocked off and it was equipped with a platform, bench and crane.

```
KELSO (Roxburgh)
Miles 359.  Map Sq. 41.
Pop. 4,119.  Clos. day Wed.
From King's Cross via Berwick.
1st cl.—Single 84/-, Return 168/-.
3rd cl.—Single 56/-, Return 112/-.
Kg's X    Kelso   Kelso   Kg's X
a.m.      a.m.    a.m.    p.m.
12 55r    10 43   8 50r   6 12
          p.m.    p.m.    a.m.
10 10r    7 36    4 40    3 3
       No Sunday Trains.
e Not Saturday.
r Refreshment Car.
s Saturday only.

Another Route
From St. Pancras or Euston via
St. Boswells.
1st cl.—Single 86/11, Return 173/10.
3rd cl.—Single 57/11, Return 115/10.
St. Pan.  Kelso   Kelso   St. Pan.
p.m.      a.m.    a.m.    p.m.
9  5e     8 40    7 35r   5§15
9§25e     8 40    10 46r  7§26
—         —       10 46r  8 15
                  p.m.
—         —       12 6sr  9§ 0
       Sunday Trains.
p.m.      a.m.
9  5      8 40    —       —
9§25      8 40    —       —

§ Euston Station.
e Not Saturday.
r Refreshment Car.
s Saturday only.
Buses from Berwick, Bus Station,
   approx. every two hours, 70-95
   min. journey.
```

From the *ABC Railway Guide*, 1956

The hub of the Tweed Valley line was Kelso. The station served, not only a town with a population of 4,119 (that was the 1956 figure), but as it was in a prime agricultural area, it consequently dealt with a fair quantity of related traffic. This picture, which was taken on 3 August 1953, shows part of the spacious goods yard on the north side of the station. To the fore is the engine shed, only one road of which is in use. The resident Sentinel, 68138, stands outside. As will be seen on the accompanying OS map, the Sentinel is standing more or less where the turntable once was. The sidings to the left of the engine shed serve the goods shed and loading dock, while in the distance on the right are the coal drops. Nowadays, all this has been swept away to accommodate the inevitable industrial estate. If there is an Institution of Industrial Estate Designers, let us hope they appreciate the contribution that Britain's railways have made to their craft! PHOTOGRAPH: J.W.ARMSTRONG TRUST

From Norham the line passed through a mix of woodland and open farmland before reaching **Twizell** (9m 43ch). This station did not appear in the public timetables until November 1861. It originally comprised just the two platform roads, the first goods siding not being laid until June 1882. In May 1885 a contractor's siding was laid on the north side of the line. A new connection between the Up line and the goods siding (which was on the Down side) was installed in August 1900, and this resulted in the original signal box – an 8-lever box which, in 1885, was reported to have all levers in use – being raised and fitted with a new 20-lever frame (16 levers in use, 4 spare).

The next station was **Coldstream** (12m 36ch). As mentioned earlier, although the town of Coldstream was in Scotland the station was on the English side of the Border in the village of Cornhill-on-Tweed. Indeed, the station was originally named Cornhill – it did not adopt its more familiar name of Coldstream until 1 October 1873. Befitting one of the most important intermediate stations on the line (relatively speaking), it had ample goods accommodation, much of it geared towards the agricultural traffic in the locality. On the east side of the station was a 50ft Cowans Sheldon turntable; it was intended principally for the tender engines on the Alnwick branch trains (q.v.) and, after those services ceased, was used for turning permanent way motor trolleys.

A Board of Trade report of November 1888 refers to the signal box at Coldstream having 24 levers (21 working, 3 spare), but by the 1920s that box had been replaced by a new stone-built box containing 38 levers (35 working, 3 spare).

Just beyond the western end of Coldstream station, the North Eastern Railway's single-track branch to Akeld, Wooler and Alnwick diverged. That said, the Alnwick branch actually paralleled the Tweed Valley line for about 600 yards before heading off on its own course. The Coldstream-Alnwick line opened throughout to passenger traffic on 5 September 1887 and, although it lost its passenger services early as 22 September 1930, it remained open to goods traffic until 1965.

Back on the Tweed Valley line and continuing westwards from Coldstream, there was once a signal box at Learmouth Siding but it closed in 1907. The next station was **Sunilaws** (15m 41ch) which first appeared in the public timetables in July 1859. It was originally named Wark, but adopted its more familiar title on 1 October 1871. Apart from the two platforms and a signal box (the original box being replaced in 1912 by a new 26-lever box), Sunilaws boasted only a coal siding and a loading dock.

A couple of miles beyond Sunilaws, the line crossed over the border from England to Scotland and shortly reached **Carham** (17m 61ch). Here there were staggered platforms with a level-crossing between them – a fairly common feature on the North Eastern system but very unusual anywhere in Scotland.

From Carham the line continued in a generally south-westerly direction on falling gradients to **Sprouston** (20m 6ch). The original signal box there was replaced in 1912 by a brick-built 'box which had 25 levers, but as early as 1926 only 13 of them were still in use. There was a small engine shed in the station yard. According to Ken Hoole's *North Eastern Locomotive Sheds*, the first shed at Sprouston was erected by the NER in 1863 at a cost of £50; it was a second-hand wooden structure from the Newcastle & Carlisle Railway. It was blown down by a gale in October 1881 but was replaced the following year by a brick building. The 'new' shed closed on 14 July 1916 – this was a wartime economy measure which was made in conjunction

Kelso station – 25-inch Ordnance Survey map of 1921 reduced to approx 17½" to the mile. The turntable was later lifted and one of the two shed roads was taken out of use. The town of Kelso is off the map to the north. CROWN COPYRIGHT

but was singled in 1933. The next station was **Roxburgh** (25m 25ch), which was also the junction for the Jedburgh branch which opened to public traffic on 17 July 1856. The Board of Trade's inspecting officer, Major-General Hutchinson, was at Roxburgh on 15 March 1886 to investigate the methods of working at the station. His report kicked off with a description of the station: *'There is a triangular platform*, with proper waiting rooms etc, for the down main line (the Tweed Valley line) and branch trains, and an up platform with waiting shed for up main line trains... Although this is a primitive station there is a bridge or subway for communicating between the platforms... There is a new raised signal cabin containing 33 working levers and 3 spare ones'.* (*The reference to a 'triangular' platform is rather misleading – the junction was 'V' shaped and there was a platform on each inner face and one outer face of the 'V'.)

As for the method of working at Roxburgh, Hutchinson reported: *'...According to the usual method now in force for working the passenger traffic between Kelso and Jedburgh, trains from Kelso are taken along the down line, about 175 yards past the platform, and then backed through the junction trailing points to the branch side of the triangular platform, where the engine runs round its train. A somewhat similar operation is performed by trains from Jedburgh on their way to Kelso. This backing of trains is not in accordance with the requirements of the Board of Trade and, moreover, involves loaded trains passing over facing points about 200 yards from the cabin...'.* The Major-General was unhappy about these arrangements, but he suggested that the situation could be eased by considerable additional interlocking of points and signals.

There were, however, other aspects of Roxburgh Junction which displeased him: *'The up main line platform is very narrow at the up end and should be widened'.* Also: *'There are two underbridges – one on the*

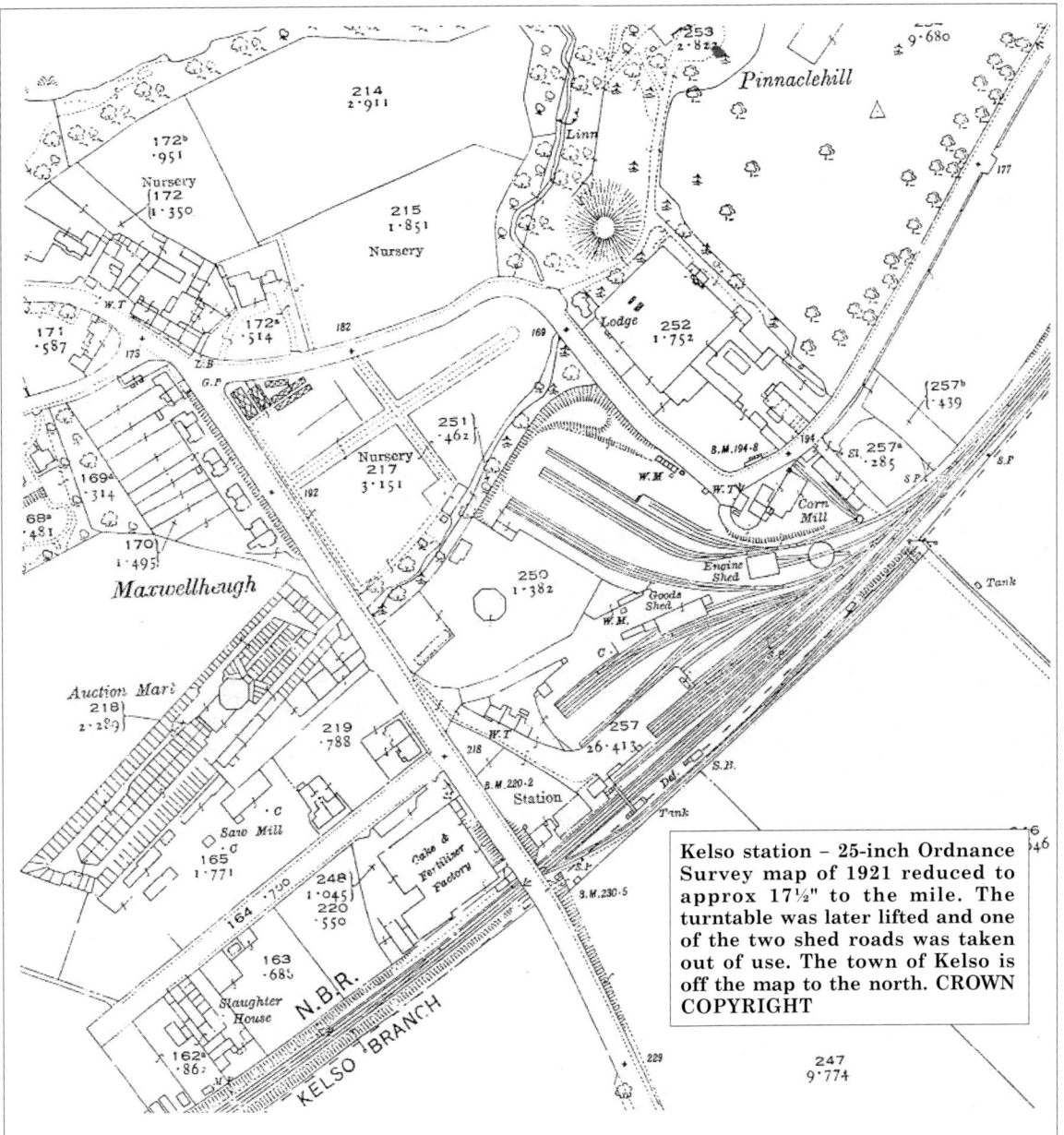

with a revision of train workings. Hitherto, the first train of the day had been from Kelso to Berwick but, under the new arrangements, the first train started at Coldstream, the engine and stock running light from Tweedmouth. At the end of the day the last train had formerly been from Tweedmouth to Kelso, but under the new arrangements the train was diverted on to the Wooler line and terminated at Alnwick.

Despite falling into disuse, Sprouston shed was left to stand and, during the Second World War, it boasted a most unusual occupant. This was none other than the celebrated GWR 4-4-0 CITY OF TRURO, which was dispatched to Sprouston as a refugee from possible bombing raids on the National Railway Museum at York. The final leg of CITY OF TRURO's journey to Sprouston was undertaken on 18 July 1941; it was towed from Tweedmouth by D49 No.220. Placing one of the nation's most historic locomotives in a safe location might seem commendable, but in this instance the authorities perhaps had not done their homework properly – during World War I there had been a Zeppelin raid at Chirnside on the Berwickshire Railway just a few miles to the north.

Just over one mile west of Sprouston the YN&B/NER section of the line ended and the NBR section commenced. Thus far, the trackside furniture had had, of course, been in the NER style – solid wooden signal posts and mileposts set at right-angles to the track (with distances from Tweedmouth) – but west of the 'junction' one inevitably found NBR lattice post signals and mileposts parallel to the line (with mileages from Edinburgh Waverley).

The first station on the NB section was **Kelso** (22m 28ch). It was by far the largest station anywhere along the line, with a bay at the rear of the down platform, a loading dock behind the up platform, a substantial goods yard and an engine shed. The shed was a two-road structure but in its later life one of the two roads was bricked off. In front of the shed there was once a 45ft turntable, but this was later removed (presumably about the time one of the shed roads was closed). The shed closed in 1955.

On leaving Kelso the railway initially climbed on a gradient of 1 in 72, but then dropped at 1 in 150 to cross the River Teviot on a beautiful, curved viaduct. As mentioned earlier, the line westwards from Kelso was originally double track

The neck of Kelso goods yard in 1963 with a pair of Standard Class 2s on manoeuvres. PHOTOGRAPH: J.W.ARMSTRONG TRUST

Standard Class 2 No.78046 at Kelso on 25 September 1961. It has arrived with the 4.00pm ex-St.Boswells and is waiting to run to the bay (with the Gresley brake compo in tow) where it will pick up a pair of vans; it will then continue to Berwick. This was a standard procedure for the 4.00. The timetables gave this train 25 minutes at Kelso – this was principally to allow for the manoeuvring but, of course, fairly lengthy waits at Kelso were part and parcel of Tweed Valley life. Indeed, when one of the authors travelled this line in the same year (1961) he found he had plenty of time to admire Kelso station. Little could be seen of the town of course, as it was well down the hill to the north, and across the Tweed. The Duke of Roxburgh had done more than anyone to nullify the value of the town's station by refusing the NBR access to his land north of the river at this point. PHOTOGRAPH: W.A.C.SMITH

NORTH BRITISH RAILWAY.

Railway Department, Board of Trade,
Whitehall, 27th May 1862.

SIR,

I AM directed by the Lords of the Committee of Privy Council for Trade to transmit to you, for the careful consideration of the Directors of the North British Railway Company, the enclosed copy of the report made by Captain Tyler, R.E., the officer appointed by my Lords to inquire into the circumstances connected with the accident which occurred on the 3rd instant to a passenger train near the Maxton station of the North British Railway.

My Lords will be glad to learn the decision which shall be come to by the Directors after considering the report made by Captain Tyler, as to the adoption of the measures recommended by that officer for ensuring the public safety.

I am, &c.
JAMES BOOTH.

The Secretary of the North British Railway Company.

---

1 *Whitehall,*
22d May 1862.

SIR,

IN compliance with the instructions contained in your minute of the 6th instant, I have the honour to report, for the information of the Lords of the Committee of Privy Council for Trade, the result of my inquiry into the circumstances which attended the accident that occurred on the 3rd instant near the Maxton station of the North British Railway.

This station is three miles to the east of the Newtown Saint Bothwell's junction, at which the Kelso branch is connected with the Edinburgh and Hawick section of the above railway. The line from Kelso to Berwick, which is in continuation of the Kelso branch, belongs to the North-eastern Company; but the North British trains run through from Edinburgh to Berwick under an arrangement between the two companies.

The 3.45 p.m. train from Edinburgh to Berwick left the Newtown junction at 5.51, four minutes late, on the day in question, consisting of an engine and tender, a loaded goods-waggon, four first- and two second-class carriages, and a break-van. It was travelling at its usual speed, stated to be under 35 miles an hour, at two miles from the Newtown junction, and one from Maxton, when the engine-driver and fireman both felt what they describe as a shake of their engine; and they observed, on looking round, that the first-class carriage second from the tender was off the rails. The engine-driver shut off his steam and the fireman applied his break, and when they looked round again they saw that some of their carriages had been left behind, and had rolled over the side of the embankment on which that part of the line runs. They brought the engine and tender to a stand after running 330 yards further, with the goods-waggon and one first-class carriage still attached to them; and they afterwards took the engine forward to Maxton to give orders for stopping a train which was nearly due at that place for Edinburgh, that it might convey a telegraph-message, to be sent forward from Newtown, for assistance.

The guard, who was riding at the tail of the train, knew nothing of what was occurring until he suddenly felt that his van was off the rails, whilst he was engaged in sorting his parcels. He was thrown down on his knees, and he caught hold of a shelf near him, and held on by it, until his van came to a stand. That vehicle and a first-class carriage in front of it remained on the top of the embankment; but the four next carriages were thrown down the side of the embankment for a depth of about 14 feet, and one of them, a second-class carriage, fourth behind the tender, was turned bottom upwards and smashed to pieces.

There were altogether about forty passengers in the train. Of these, one was unfortunately killed, three were seriously injured, and eighteen or twenty others are returned as having suffered from internal injuries, bruises, cuts, &c. The passenger who lost his life, and those who were the most injured, were riding in the second-class carriage above referred to. One axle from under that carriage was broken, and the other was much bent, no doubt from the violent treatment that it received after it left the rails, and as it was pitched over the side of the embankment. The bent axle and the wheels attached to it were torn from the axleguards, and the only wheel left in its place was that which was detached from the broken axle. That wheel has received a tremendous blow, which has fractured the tyre, and forced off the head of one of the rivets by which it was secured to the rim, in somewhat altering its shape. The axle and the other wheel were amongst the wreck, and no portion was left behind to indicate that any failure occurred in the rolling stock before it was thrown off the line and subjected to so much violence. The axles of the other carriages were all slightly bent.

The dimensions of the broken axle were $3\frac{7}{8}''$ in diameter in the centre, $3\frac{3}{4}''$ in the boss of the wheel, and $2\frac{1}{2}''$ by $5''$ in the journal. It had no previous flaw in it, but was an old axle, and of smaller dimensions than would now be constructed for a passenger carriage.

It will have been observed that out of the whole train the engine and tender only remained on the rails, and that, of the eight vehicles behind them, four were thrown down the embankment, the two first having followed the engine and tender till they were pulled up, and the two last having come to a stand by themselves on the bank. These latter were found to be nearly opposite the wreck of the carriages below.

The engine, No. 187, belonged to the North-eastern Company, and was a six-wheeled engine, with the middle and trailing wheels coupled together. The cylinders were $15''$ in diameter, with a $22''$ stroke. The weights on the leading, driving, and trailing wheels were 10 tons 5 cwt., 11 tons 0 cwt., and 7 tons 0 cwt. respectively. The diameter of the leading wheels was $3'\ 8''$, and that of the other wheels was $6'\ 1\frac{1}{4}''$. The total wheel-base was $14'\ 3''$, made up of $7'\ 3''$ between the leading and driving, and $7'\ 0''$ between the driving and trailing axles. The cylinders were inside the framing, and the engine was attached to the tender by means of a central screw coupling and buffer, without side buffers, but with safety chains, so that it would have gone round the curve with comparative freedom.

The permanent way was about thirteen years old, and was laid with double-headed rails, 16 feet long, weighing 75 lbs. to the lineal yard, and resting in cast-iron chairs. The joints were not fished; the chairs were supported on transverse sleepers, $3'\ 2\frac{2}{3}''$ apart on the average from centre to centre, and they were attached to them by means of wooden trenails, three to each joint chair and two to each intermediate chair. The train had descended a gradient of 1 in 100, and had run on the level for rather more than 200 yards before the first disturbance observed in the road. It was travelling round a curve of 60 chains radius, and iron spikes had been driven into some of the chairs, but not into all of them, on the outside of this curve.

The first disturbance noticed was, that a rail on the right was slightly bulged outwards towards the right or outside of the curve; the next, that a rail in front of this was bent outwards on the left or inside of the curve; and a few yards further forward another rail on the right was very considerably bent outwards. This last rail had evidently been held fast by the joint chair at each end, and by an intermediate chair next the joint at the west end, while the fastenings of the other three chairs supporting it must have given way. From this point forward there were some very decided marks on the chairs on the inside of the curve, as if the flanges of the wheels had there got over the inside rail, while the chairs under the outside rail had been broken, as would appear by their having been replaced by new ones; and 20 or 30 yards beyond there were wheel-marks on one of the sleepers. From this point forward the wheel-marks were distinctly traceable over the sleepers when I visited the spot on the 15th instant, and the road appeared to have been more or less torn up, as a result of the accident. At 68 yards only from the first disturbance the four carriages in the middle of the train left the ballast, and 50 yards further forward they lay at the bottom of the embankment.

The chairs which came from the parts of the line at which new chairs had been inserted, could not be particularly identified, any more than the sleepers; and the evidence as to the precise condition in which the permanent way was found to be after the accident was not as satisfactory as I could have wished; but, from the position of the bent rails, the new chairs, and the new fastenings, and from the best information that I could obtain when on the spot, I have no doubt that the accident occurred in consequence of the failure of the trenails which ought to have secured the chairs to the sleepers.

The engine appears in its passage along the line to have bulged the rails, first to the right, then to the left, then considerably to the right; and thus to have so far disturbed the permanent way as to cause the vehicles behind it to be thrown off the line. The "shake" of the engine when this occurred was noticed both by the engine driver and by the fireman, and was, indeed, sufficient to cause them to look back. They only observed, as I have stated, that a first-class carriage was off the rails. The waggon in front of it may either have left the rails at the same time, or may have been pulled off them afterwards by the carriages.

I observe that the sleepers on this line are being now altogether renewed, which they require, and that some of them had been renewed before the accident; and I recommend that the joints should be fished and the line thoroughly ballasted without delay, as well as that all the trenails should be replaced by iron spikes.

After the many reports that I have had occasion to make to their Lordships within the last few years, particularly on the 25th May in last year, and the 5th April and 29th April in the present year, on the subject of accidents that have occurred in consequence of the treacherous character of wooden trenails used for securing the chairs to the sleepers in the permanent way of railways, and the observations contained in these reports, I need not now do more than draw attention to the circumstance that this is another lamentable instance of the insecurity of these fastenings.

I have the honour to be, Sir,
Your obedient Servant,
H. W. TYLER,
Captain, Royal Engineers.

The Secretary, Board of Trade, Whitehall.

main line and the other on the branch near the up end of the platform, the parapets of which should be provided with hand rails to prevent passengers from accidentally stepping over into the road below'. The NBR seemed in no hurry to execute the Major-General's requirements, as it was 27 October 1887 before the alterations finally received the 'all clear'.

The Jedburgh branch was a casualty of the floods of 1948 (more of which anon), its last ordinary passenger services running on 12 August, but after the flood damage had been repaired its goods services were reinstated and lasted for another ten years. They were withdrawn as from Monday 10 August 1964; latterly, there had been one train each day, Mondays to Saturdays.

Continuing on the Tweed Valley line from Roxburgh there was a two-mile climb of 1 in 150 to **Rutherford** (28m 31ch), a very modest little station with its buildings about 50 yards from the platform. There was a temporary signal box at Rutherford from April to July 1898. Then it was on to **Maxton** (30m 73ch). This was another small station; it was provided with a signal box in 1915 but in February 1932 the box was relegated to the status of a gate box. However, it was reinstated as a block post on 3 November 1942 (this was in connection with the opening of a siding to the Air Ministry siding at Charlesfield – see later) and, somewhat extravagantly, remained open until 29 March 1965, by which time the branch – or what was left of it – was worked on the 'one engine in steam' principle.

Beyond Maxton the line was fairly level. It was on this stretch of line that, on 3 May 1862, the 3.45pm Edinburgh-St.Boswells-Kelso-Berwick mixed train left the rails. Although the engine, tender, brake van and two of the carriages remained upright, the other four carriages were thrown down a 14ft embankment. Of the forty passengers in the toppled carriages, one was killed, three were seriously injured but, somewhat miraculously, the others all escaped with nothing more than cuts and bruises. The accident was routinely investigated by the Board of Trade and it was concluded that the cause was '...the failure of the wooden trenails which ought to have secured the chairs to the sleepers'. The author of the report, Captain Tyler, opined that '...this was another lamentable instance of the insecurity of these fastenings'.

About two miles beyond Maxton on the west side of the line was the Air Ministry factory at Charlesfield which opened in 1942. The factory had a siding connected to the Tweed Valley line, a loop capable of holding 60 wagons, and engine and brake van, being provided alongside the Tweed Valley line itself. The factory closed in 1946 but was later taken over by the Ministry of Supply and, in 1949, was reopened by the Admiralty as an armaments depot. In this guise it remained operational until 1961. An RNAD diesel shunter was employed at the depot. Charlesfield depot had a a halt on the Waverley Route; if that halt had been built on the Tweed Valley line instead

LNER Southern Scottish Area WTT, July 1930 to May 1931

BERWICK and KELSO — Weekdays

Col	1	4	5	6	7	8	9	10	13	14	15	16	17	21	22	23	24
Type	D Goods	PASSENGER	D Goods			PASSENGER Steam Coach	Engine and Van	PASSENGER		B Cattle Empties	PASSENGER Steam Coach	D Goods	A	PASSENGER	PASSENGER	D Goods	Light Engine	PASSENGER
Notes	Q					FOQ			FOQ		SX	MO Q			SO	AltMO	

DOWN (Distance from Berwick, M.C.):

Station	1	4	5	8	9	10	13	14	15	16	17	21	22	23	24
BERWICK dep	S a.m.	6 5	E a.m.	H a.m.		G a.m.	W a.m.		H a.m.	11 40			B p.m. 2 15	E p.m.	T p.m. 6 30
1 12 Tweedmouth	5 0	6 8	6 14	7 30	8 14	8 48	8 52	11 10	11 43	11 49	12 15	12 35	2 18	2 24	4 10		4 32	5 19	5 33	5 39
5 22 Velvet Hall	5 13 A 23		6 22	7 39		9 0				11 58	12 28	12 48		2 32	4 18		4 45	5 0		5 47
7 65 Norham			6 27	7 44		9 5				12 3	12 57	1 17		2 37	4 23		5 9	5 25		5 52
10 55 Twizell	A		6 32	7 50		9 10				12 9	1 26	1 35		2 42	4 28		5 45			5 57
13 48 Coldstream	5 52	6 17	6 38	6 41	7 10	7 30	7 56	8 35	9 16	9 17	11 40		12 16	1 45	2 15	6	2 48	2 49	4 34	5 55	6 30	5 35	6 3	6 4
16 53 Sunilaws		A		7 41	7 A 43		8 43	9 23			12 23	2 26	2 36		2 55		6 48	6 57		6 10
18 74 Carham	6 3	6 A 44		Alnwick 8.12 a.m. p.3			9 28			12 28	2 44	3 •6		3 0		7 5	7 18		6 15
21 18 Sprouston	A						9 32			12 33	3 13	3 18		3 4		7 19	7 26		6 19
23 40 Kelso	6 55	—		8 8		9 37			Wooler 12.24 p.m. p.3	12 38		3 21		1 25	3 9	Alnwick 6.0 vm. p.3	7 34		5 55	6 24	6 36

B — West Ord Siding A.   D.P.M.   S — Class B from Coldstream.   Learmouth Siding A.   T — St. Boswell's arr. 6.57 p.m.   E — See note E page 3.   V — Does not run when No 1 is running.   G — "H" except from one intermediate station to St. Boswell's and beyond by arrangement with D.P.M.   W — Alnwick dep. 7.20 a.m., p.10.

UP (Distance from Kelso, M.C.):

Col	1	2	3	4	5	6	8	9	10	13	15	16	17	19	20	21	22	23	24
Type	Goods and Cattle	PASSENGER Steam Coach		Goods	B Cattle	PASSENGER	PASSENGER Steam Coach	EXPRESS PASSENGER	B Goods	PASSENGER	D Cattle	D Goods	D Cattle	A Cattle	PASSENGER		PASSENGER	D Goods	
Notes	Q				FOQ						MOQ	SX	FOQ	AltMO				SO	

Station	1	2	4	5	6	8	9	10	13	15	16	17	19	20	22	23
Kelso dep	J a.m. 7 20	H a.m.	JK a.m. 8 49		9 55		12 55			3 25				4 0	6 20	6 50		8 20
2 22 Sprouston	A	—	A		10 0	1 0				3 30	4 7	4 17	4 22	4 27		6 56		8 27	8 55
4 46 Carham	A		A		10 5	1 5				3 35	4 24	4 34	4 34	4 43		7 1		8 42	8 55
6 67 Sunilaws	A		A	3 50	10 10	1 10				3 40	4 42	4 58	4 51	5 15		7 6		9 5	9 20
9 72 Coldstream	7 40	8 10	9 0	10 10	10 20	10 16	10 21	1 17	3 18	2 43	3 30	3 46	3 48	5 1	5 25	6 20	6 20	7 0	7 12	7 13	8 14	9 30	9 52
12 65 Twizell	Wooler 9.45 a.m.	8 16	Wooler 12.18 p.m. p.3	10 40	10 45		10 27			3 40	4 5			5 30	6 35			7 19	8 20	10 19	
15 55 Norham		8 23		10 58	11 5		10 33	1 29		4 15	4 32			4 0	6 45	7 2	6 35	6 45	7 25	8 26	10 38
18 18 Velvet Hall		8 29		11 15	11 45		10 39	1 35		4 42	5 1			4 6		7 12	7 43	6 57	3	7 31	8 32	10 48	10 58
22 28 Tweedm'th		8 1/40		11 40		10 46	10 51	1 43	1 47	3 36	5 16			4 13	4 18	5 30		8 3	Alnwick 6.45 p.m. p.3	7 18	7 38	7 43	8 39	11 18
23 40 BERWICK	p. 3	8 43	p. 3	—	—	—	10 54	1 50	—	—	—	4 21	—	—	—	—	—	7 46	—		

B — St. Boswells dep. 5.55 p.m.   J — Works Carham Tile Works. Shunts Sprouston Siding.   K — Does not run when No. 1 is running.   S — Class B from Sunilaws.   W — When No. 17 is running, leaves Coldstream 6.30 p.m. and runs correspondingly later.   x — Arr. 6 A 50 p.m.   y — Arr. 8.37 a.m.

---

there could well have been a couple of workmen's trains on the Kelso line each day. About a mile beyond the Charlesfield siding, the Tweed Valley line joined the Waverley Line at the appropriately named Kelso Junction. A Board of Trade report dated 1880 stated that the signal box at the junction had 14 levers; following the extension of the branch loop at the junction in November 1942 the box had 25 levers (19 working, 6 spare). From the junction, the Tweed Valley trains continued along the main line to terminate at St.Boswells (a total of 33 miles 74 chains from Tweedmouth station), where they used a bay at the south end of the station.

Trains and services

Going back to the early days of the Tweed Valley line, although the junction between the YN&B and the NBR sections was nearer to Sprouston, Kelso became the 'frontier' station. From the outset the train services were hardly prolific, the YN&B offering only three trains daily in 1854, one of which had no third class accommodation. Fares between Tweedmouth and Kelso ranged from 4/6d First Class to 2/6d Third Class, with return fares calculated at single rate plus one-sixth – a not ungenerous fare. Sunday services were a feature of the line – or at least part of it – from very early on. By 1861 (if not before) the timetables advertised two trains between Berwick and Kelso on Sundays – not only during the summer, but year-round.

For periods of the line's life a curious, and ultimately moribund, aspect of timetabling was the reluctance of both companies to treat it operationally as a through route. But there was at least a degree of co-operation which benefited the companies, if not their passengers. This is confirmed by the YN&B minute books which reveal that, on 11 June 1852, the directors '…read a letter stating that the Directors of the North British Company were of the opinion that the line between Tweedmouth and St.Boswells might be more economically worked by one set of engines than by each company working their own proportion…'.

It appears that the NBR's overtures to the YN&B in 1852 had some effect, as the Board of Trade report into an accident near Maxton in May 1862 stated that the North British train involved in the incident was being worked by North Eastern Railway 2-4-0 No.187. Furthermore, the same BoT report stated that '…North British trains run through from Edinburgh to Berwick under an arrangement between the two companies'.

It will be noted that the foregoing BoT report mentioned a North Eastern train. The North Eastern Railway had come into existence on 31 July 1854, the product of the old York Newcastle & Berwick Railway's amalgamation with three other companies.

Early passengers soon learned the reality of cross-Border travel on the line. We know this from the diary of John Hutton Balfour, Professor of Botany at Edinburgh University, who brought a party of fifteen to Kelso one July evening in 1857 to 'botanise' along the course of the Tweed. They held NBR return tickets taking them from Edinburgh to Kelso and then from Berwick back northwards on the main-line, all for 3/6d each. However, to progress beyond Kelso they had to purchase single tickets from there to Cornhill – for a shilling, not much of a bargain – whence they walked to Coldstream, where they put up for the night in no fewer than three inns and the local manse. Next day the botanists rose early and began a 7-hour walk along the Tweed, cheerfully uprooting any plant which caught their interest (this is illegal nowadays), and reaching Norham in mid-afternoon. The train fare from here on to Berwick was 1/2d each, and the travellers, now laden with gradually-expiring specimens, caught a northbound train.

Twelve years later, Professor Balfour was back with no fewer than 49 companions, a party which must have made an impressive sight on their arrival at the modest wayside station of Twizell. Naturally, they had been forced to break their journey at Kelso, using the delay there to eat a hearty meal. After 'botanising' their way through two local estates near Twizell, the group walked to Berwick where they caught what the diary calls 'the London express' at 7pm, arriving at Edinburgh 90 minutes later.

In any event, it was not just lengthy sojourns at Kelso which constituted the problem – the timetabling there was also

LNER North Eastern Area WTT, 1 May 1939 u.f.n.

a little eccentric. As late as 1920, when it should have been obvious to rail managers that they were going to need all the passengers they could find on a line with only light freight traffic, some trains were being timetabled out of Kelso a few minutes before the arrival of the connecting service from either east or west.

The timing of connections also affected the Jedburgh branch, and this prompted Jedburgh Town Council to complain to the Ministry of Transport. In their letter (of 1920), the council informed the BoT that the 9.31am out of their town reached Kelso three minutes after a train departed for the ECML at Tweedmouth or Berwick-on-Tweed. Similarly, the 6.48pm westwards was pathed out of

A C15 (possibly 67477) waits at Kelso with a Tweedmouth-bound train on 26 April 1952. A St.Boswells-bound train stands at the other platform. Given the very sparse passenger patronage of the line, the length of the station platforms – the one on the right seems to have been extended at some time during its life – was a case of serious over-provision. The bridge at the far end of the station carries the B6352 Kelso-Kirk Yetholm road. PHOTOGRAPH: J.W.ARMSTRONG TRUST

G5 No.67268 takes water at Kelso while waiting with the 3.28pm Berwick-St.Boswells on 12 June 1954. PHOTOGRAPH: W.A.C.SMITH

Roxburgh Junction, looking towards St.Boswells. The line from Kelso comes in from the right and the Jedburgh branch from the left. We see LNER signal arms on NBR lattice posts. PHOTOGRAPH: KEITH FENWICK

C15 No.67457 waits at Kelso with a St.Boswells-Berwick train *circa* 1952. PHOTOGRAPH: K.H.COCKERILL; COURTESY J.W.ARMSTRONG TRUST

Kelso seven minutes before the arrival of a train from the east. NBR files in the Scottish Record Office show (sadly) that the company was able to *justify* these timings to the satisfaction of the Ministry.

The public timetables for the summer of 1922 – the last summer before the Grouping – listed what were, in theory, three through trains from Tweedmouth to St.Boswells and two in the opposite direction on weekdays. There were additional workings between Tweedmouth and Coldstream (these continued to/from the Alnwick branch) and between Kelso and St.Boswells. All but two of the trains to/from Tweedmouth continued to/from Berwick. The Sunday service comprised two trains each way between Berwick and Kelso only.

With the North British and the North Eastern both coming into the LNER fold at the Grouping in 1923, co-ordination of services, not only on the Tweed Valley line itself, but also in conjunction with the St.Boswells-Reston Junction line, should have been perfectly possible, but was not practised. Quite the opposite, in fact. Trains were scheduled to leave St.Boswells for each line at exactly the same time on no less than three occasions each day, when it would have been simpler for a service from Tweedmouth, having stopped at St.Boswells, to have headed back to Berwick via Duns and Reston Junction. But this opportunity to rationalise manpower and equipment usage, while increasing train frequency on both lines, was not undertaken. As one commentator put it: 'The LNER management seemed content to leave the old protagonists to their own devices'.

Untypical co-operation

In 1926 there was an incident which clearly showed that, in an emergency, cross-Border co-operation was perfectly practicable and, indeed, was unselfishly rendered on either side. All the more reason to be baffled at the lack of timetabling co-ordination as a matter of routine! This incident of 1926 is worth examining in detail.

At the end of June of that year the Highland and Agricultural Society of Scotland was considering venues for its annual show, but Kelso was in competition with Hawick and Peebles for the event. The last-named was chosen as the 1926 site by the Society, but a press report suggested that the LNER's Area Superintendent, Major Stemp, had recommended that Kelso was a logistical non-starter. This created huge protest in the lower Tweed Valley, Kelso councillors pointing out that the show had not visited there since 1898, when the NBR had been described as having no problems in the handling of passengers as well as livestock and machinery. Even the LNER's first chairman, William Whitelaw (a former NBR man), was drawn into the controversy, having to counsel his staff – 'The thing wants careful handling', was his advice – while publicly denying that the LNER was dictating agricultural policy.

Stemp's objection to Kelso was purely logistical; previous attendance figures, and more specifically the number of livestock wagons required, suggested that the traffic would overwhelm the town's rail facilities. The loading bays were certainly not going to be able to cope with up to 500 cattle wagons to be loaded by 3.00am on the morning after the show closed, and passenger facilities were little better, there being only one ladies' toilet at the station. The previous year's show had attracted 58,000 spectators, so Major Stemp's problem can be easily seen.

The nettle had to be grasped when a landowner at Peebles changed his mind about allowing the Society access, so Kelso it was. The LNER had estimated that £1,500 would have to be spent on temporary facilities, principally a loading bay on a running line (and on a 1 in 75 gradient). In the event, the work was done for less than half that amount. Archival papers give no hint as to whether the railway sought any kind of compensation or guarantees to cover for this, but the new loading bank became a permanent fixture.

The number of livestock wagons processed during the Show came to 295, all of them despatched by 3.15 on the morning after the event. 752 wagon loads of equipment were handled – twice – and all this within a five-day period, and 11,407 passenger tickets were sold, with a turnover of £5,267.7.3d. These were of course for double journeys, meaning that around 5,500 people had travelled by rail. Overall attendance was approximately 49,000, showing that, even as early as the mid-1920s, the railway company was losing traffic to road. Indeed, one local transport concern had boasted to the Border newspapers that it would put forty buses on the road to cater for Show traffic.

An unforeseen complication was a royal presence at the Show, the Prince of Wales arriving at Berwick on an overnight train. He was sent on to Kelso by special. Offers were made to take train rakes for storage east of Sprouston whenever required, and all locomotives on westbound trips were watered before entering the Kelso area. Weather conditions on the final day posed an additional problem – flash-flooding covered the line above rail height at one time.

To summarise this almost unique chapter in the Tweed Valley line's history, it is worth quoting from Stemp's telegram to Edinburgh HQ at the conclusion of the event: *'Royal special arrived here sharp to time. All well. Working yesterday excellent and Duke of Roxburgh and Highland [Society] directors express great satisfaction about 5,000 passengers hauled, and all trains, including long distance, arrived sharp on time or before'*.

If nothing else, the railway operations for the Show had proved that the LNER's North Eastern Area and Scottish Area (the old NER and NBR sections) could co-operate and, to all outward appearances, work as one. But this had been for a special event – the ordinary public services did not benefit from the same level of corporate camaraderie.

Shunting at Kelso
A further word about Kelso… For most of the Tweed Valley line's life the goods yard at Kelso was usually very busy, but some of the sidings were too sharply curved for locomotive working so, for many years, the shunting was undertaken by a horse (known to the local railwaymen as the 'hairy pilot'). However, following the easing of the sharpest curves, in February 1921 locomotive power replaced horse power. The locomotive was a petrol-engined Simplex which the NBR had purchased specifically for use at Kelso. The NBR rule book stated the Simplex was prohibited from the 'main line' and was 'intended to haul a maximum of 5 wagons'. The staff presumably adhered to the 'not on the main line' rule, but the 'maximum of five wagons' was often ignored. However, despite often being grossly overburdened, the little Simplex soldiered on at Kelso until 1928. Perhaps surprisingly, the annual cost of locomotive working at Kelso goods was cheaper than horse working – the locomotive ran up bills of £904 p.a. whereas the horses had cost £1,180. Even allowing for the £121 it had cost the NBR to ease the curves, it was a worthwhile economy.

The Simplex had its hardest tests during 1926 when Kelso had to deal with the vast quantity of traffic for the Highland and Agricultural Society Show (mentioned earlier). It seems that it did not cope too well – but it had hardly been designed for such a work-load – and shunting operations at Kelso were subsequently discussed at the very highest level in the LNER echelons. The outcome was the arrival, in July 1928, of a 100hp Sentinel locomotive, LNER No.9529. The Sentinel eventually became BR No.68138 and remained at Kelso (albeit nominally allocated to the parent shed at Hawick, where it went for wash-outs and routine maintenance) until August 1955 when, following the closure of Kelso shed, it was transferred to Ayr.

Singling
As mentioned earlier the Tweed Valley line had been singled between Kelso and Kelso Junction (the junction with the Waverley Line near St.Boswells) in 1933. However, following the outbreak of the Second World War the authorities realised that, if the East Coast Main Line should be put out of action by the enemy (there was particular concern about the Royal Border Bridge at Berwick being hit), the Tweed Valley line could be used as a diversionary route. Consequently, various improvements were made to the Tweed Valley line should it be needed for such a purpose. The crossing loop at Roxburgh was extended to provide a clear length of 490 yards (this was brought into use on 15 December 1942), a 450-yard-long crossing loop was constructed at Maxton (brought into use on 3 November 1942)

Tweedmouth's J39 No.64917 trundles westwards through Maxton with a train of hopper wagons on 26 August 1960. This would not have been a local train, so we assume that it was an ECML working which had been diverted for some reason or other. As for Maxton itself, the line through the station had originally been double track but had been singled in 1933. However, a 450-yard long passing loop was laid in 1942 (this is the line on the right - note the plethora of concrete pots in lieu of 'proper' sleepers) though, as is clearly evident here, the second platform was *not* reinstated. PHOTOGRAPH: HUGH BALLANTYNE

In the mid-1950s the V1 and V3 2-6-2Ts were regular performers on the Tweed Valley line. This is St.Margarets-based 67630 – one which was never rebuilt as a V3 – waiting at Kelso with the 4.05pm St.Boswells-Berwick on 6 May 1957. PHOTOGRAPH: HUGH BALLANTYNE

and the double-track portion of the branch at Kelso Junction was extended by 210 yards (also brought into use on 3 November 1942). As noted earlier, the changes resulted in Maxton being reinstated as a block post.

The new sections of track were laid with '92lb second-hand NB-type rails on new sleepers and slag ballast'. The frames at three signal boxes had to be altered: Roxburgh Junction box now had 40 working levers and 2 spare, Maxton had 21 working levers and 1 spare (plus the gate wheel), while Kelso Junction box now had 19 working levers and 6 spare plus 2 detonator slides.

Motive power – pre-BR

In pre-Grouping days the motive power for the NER section of the Tweed Valley line was supplied from Tweedmouth and its sub-shed at Sprouston, while NBR motive power came from St.Boswells (in later years a sub of Hawick) and its own outstation at Kelso. After the Grouping those sheds and sub-sheds all came into the LNER fold, but the 'separateness' was still very evident, with each section continuing to rely largely on native types.

The line saw regular appearances from tender locomotives: D20 4-4-0s and J21 0-6-0s from the English side, with North British 4-4-0s of the D30, D31, D32 and D33 classes from the St.Boswells end. Other classes which appeared less frequently included D1s, D26s, D29s, D34s, D49s, K3 2-6-0s, J36s and J37s.

In LNER days former North Eastern 4-4-0s would often work through to Galashiels on the Waverley Route. Given that the Tweed Valley line was R.A.6 (with dispensation for R.A.9 engines), and that the Berwickshire line, a little to the north, was also R.A.6, there would have been nothing to have stopped the LNER 4-4-0s, or any other locomotives, from working home from St.Boswells via the Berwickshire Railway, forming a near-circle on Tweedmouth.

Despite the use of tender engines, most of the regular passenger services were usually handled by tank engines. The North Eastern used its Worsdell 'O' class (later LNER G5) 0-4-4Ts on its services as far as Kelso. One of the class was stationed at Sprouston for many years. The NBR and later LNER – and, even later, BR – used C15 4-4-2Ts.

In 1930s the early morning Berwick-Coldstream and return and the late morning Berwick-Kelso and return were diagrammed for a Sentinel steam railmotor. The railmotor which handled these jobs was ROYAL CHARLOTTE, one of the 100hp versions, which went new to Tweedmouth in August 1929 and remained until March 1941. When that car was unavailable the usual substitute was HERO.

An interesting working on Saturdays in 1943 involved a Heaton-based ex-NER C7 4-4-2. Its diagram started with the 7.15am Newcastle-Berwick, after which it worked the 12.10pm Tweedmouth-Coldstream and return before heading home with the 3.15pm ex-Berwick.

Services – 1930s and 1940s

It can be seen from the accompanying WTT for the winter of 1930/31 (page 14) that there were, at that time, still only four passenger trains between Tweedmouth and Kelso on weekdays. All but one of those ran through to/from Berwick. The Tweedmouth-Coldstream section was also served by local trains plus trains to/from Wooler or Alnwick. Paths were provided for various goods and cattle trains, though most were conditional.

By 1939 there had been a number of changes; some of those affecting the Tweedmouth-Coldstream locals were a consequence of the Alnwick branch's closure to passengers in 1930. The summer timetables for 1939 showed that many of the actual timings of the trains had changed, and that there was now an additional Saturdays Only evening railmotor each way (9.25pm Berwick-Kelso, 10.30pm return). There was also an 'express passenger' (that's what the WTT says) on Sundays: 10.30am ex-Newcastle to Tweedmouth, Kelso, St.Boswells and on to Edinburgh (arr.2.14pm). The return working left Edinburgh at 5.45pm and, running via

Kelso, was scheduled to arrive back at Newcastle at 9.38pm. By this time the ordinary Sunday services ran only during the summer. The timetables for March 1940 advertised three trains each way between Tweedmouth and Kelso and one between Tweedmouth and Coldstream (all of these ran through to/from Berwick). The St.Boswells-Kelso section was served by six each way on Mondays-Fridays and eight on Saturdays. For anyone wishing to travel from St.Boswells to Tweedmouth a few of the waits at Kelso were vaguely bearable, but the only services actually flagged in the timetables as through trains were the 5.25pm Berwick-St.Boswells (arr. 6.50pm) and the 5.57pm St.Boswells-Berwick (arr.7.40pm). The Kelso-Roxburgh section was also served by three trains each way to/from Jedburgh (the other Jedburgh trains started or terminated at Roxburgh). The services for the early post-war period were very similar.

Floods

Earlier we saw that, although the Tweed Valley line was normally operated as two separate sections, the two Divisions had pulled together for the Highland and Agricultural Society Show at Kelso in 1926. In 1948 there was another noteworthy incident which showed that inter-Regional co-operation could be achieved on the line, if only there were the will or a desperate enough need. This was to do with flooding – but not just any old flooding.

Although it might be thought more appropriate for a meteorological periodical than one dealing with railway history, a brief account of the 1948 Floods is necessary here as it underlined the strategic importance of the Tweed Valley line – an importance greater than its traffic-carrying statistics, real or potential. The facts are that rainfall had already been heavy in the Scottish Borders in the first week of August 1948, but on Thursday 12th, phenomenal weather conditions occurred. 400 million tons of water fell on the Tweed Valley in a 24-hour period, equivalent to more than five inches of rain over an area of 130 square miles. Streams and rivers were turned into torrents and embankments took on the consistency of melting chocolate. Older residents still recall the sight of animal carcasses floating past their houses. It was a miracle that no human life was lost.

The area's railways were overwhelmed. The East Coast main line was cut in thirteen places, with seven bridges swept away and six landslips. The Waverley Route suffered four landslides, while the St.Boswells-Duns and Jedburgh branches were so badly damaged that they lost their passenger services forever, the former of these two branches being cut in two and never re-connected. The Tweed Valley line escaped surprisingly lightly considering it was in the centre of the storm; the only real damage was a landslip at Carham. Once this was repaired, rail managers were able to look at the line as a useful deviation for the ECML which, it was quickly realised, was to be out of action for the best part of three months.

With the repair at Carham being very quickly completed, the Tweed Valley line reopened throughout just four days after the disaster, it was possible to route such East Coast expresses as the Flying Scotsman – scheduled to be non-stop between Edinburgh (Waverley) and London (King's Cross) – via the Waverley Route and the Tweed Valley. What happened next was an extraordinary passage of improvisatory railroading excellence: express enginemen decided that 'Non Stop' should be exactly that, even if meant breaking records!

Previously, the British record for a journey without stops had been set up by the LMS over the 401 miles between Euston and Glasgow (Central), but BR's diversionary route between Kings Cross and Edinburgh via the Tweed Valley line was some seven miles longer. It required crews to zealously husband their water supplies as, after leaving Edinburgh, the first water troughs were 88 miles away at Lucker in Northumberland. Southbound trains, faced with a trying gradient of nearly ten miles up Falahill bank, had no prospect of 'rushing' the climb, and the Tweed Valley line had to be negotiated at no more than 25 mph.

In the circumstances, just getting through should have been enough, but a number of Top Link drivers thought differently. The decision to run non-stop did not come from on high – it was made in the engine-crews' mess-room and on the footplate. Seventeen such trips were made between 24 August and 18 September, eight of them northbound, when the A4s concerned had already clocked 300 miles without a break.

In the book *Non-Stop!*, this author discussed the attempt by Haymarket

In the early 1960s the Standard Class 2s took over most of the remaining Tweed Valley passenger services. By this time the trains usually comprised only one coach – and that provided far more accommodation than was ever necessary. On 31 May 1962 No.78047 was in charge of the 9.56am Berwick-St.Boswells, the train comprising a solitary Gresley brake compo. This picture was taken on the western outskirts of Tweedmouth. PHOTOGRAPH: MICHAEL MENSING

Ivatt 2-6-0 No.46482 with the pick-up goods at Coldstream, 1 June 1962. The engine is moving on to wagons which had been collected from the goods yard; the ensemble will be taken on to Kelso. The 'V' near the bottom of the middle panel on the 8-plank wagon indicates that it is a hopper. PHOTOGRAPH: MICHAEL MENSING

drivers to bring the non-stop *Flying Scotsman* through the 1948 floods by the Tweed Valley line. It was generally assumed that 9 September was the date of the final non-stop trip northbound, as related by the late O.S.Nock, but subsequent evidence suggests otherwise. On the 21st of the month, Alan Robinson, a young clerk in BR's CME department at Derby, was taking advantage of his travel privilege, journeying to Edinburgh via London on the famous train. He records his memories thus: *'Whilst I shudder at the very thought of contradicting O.S.Nock, we did have a non-stop run on the 21st [September], via Kelso, behind No.60024 KINGFISHER. As a callow youth of 17 I did not have the gravitas to ask for the names of the crew! That day remains as one of the highlights of my love affair with railways. I did not record the arrival time [at Waverley] – my memory is of just after 7pm [rescheduled arrival time]. Certainly I was walking around Haymarket shed at 7.45pm according to my notes'.*

Interestingly, the 'red' emergency timetable which was made available to the travelling public in September 1948 not only announced new timings for ECML expresses – with Tweedmouth deputising for Berwick-on-Tweed for those stopping at the border town – but also intimated the withdrawal of stopping trains between St.Boswells and Kelso during the emergency. Effectively, this meant the temporary closure of the stations at Maxton, Rutherford, and Roxburgh Junction. Users of the wayside stations east of Kelso were luckier; their services appear to have continued almost without interruption.

Mention was made of Roxburgh Junction. The floods resulted in its junction role being permanently over; the Jedburgh branch had temporarily closed to passengers, but it was not reopened. 'Jeddart' trains were now shown as starting or finishing their journeys at Kelso. Another casualty was the branch between Coldstream, Wooler and Alnwick.

The floods severed this line south of Wooler and it was subsequently worked as two unconnected sections: Coldstream-Wooler and Alnwick-Ilderton. The Coldstream-Wooler section was served by a daily goods from Coldstream.

Even after the East Coast Main Line was back to normal, some goods trains were still routed via the Tweed Valley line. For example, in 1950 the 7.00am Niddrie-Tweedmouth, 10.45am Portobello-Tweedmouth, 8.45am Tweedmouth-Meadows (Edinburgh) and 2.00pm Tweedmouth-Meadows were all routed via Kelso.

BR days

When conditions returned to normal after the floods, the traditional – almost grudging – level of services resumed, and was perpetuated during the 1950s and 1960s. Although the Tweed Valley line was traversed by various excursion trains throughout the year, most ran through to and from Newcastle or seaside resorts in

Class 2 No.78048 prepares to pull away from Coldstream with the 9.56am Berwick-St.Boswells on 1 June 1962. PHOTOGRAPH: MICHAEL MENSING

the north-east. Comparatively few of the excursions were specifically for towns along the Tweed Valley; this was perhaps an opportunity lost as 'River Tweed' specials from Edinburgh, Newcastle or Carlisle, with breaks at Kelso or Norham for tourists to visit their historical ruins, could have been rather popular. Kelso continued to be regarded as an outpost between two systems; this had hardly been appropriate after the Grouping in 1923, let alone in the 1950s. If nothing else, the Scottish Region public timetables listed the services on the whole line – St.Boswells right through to Tweedmouth and Berwick. But the North Eastern Region timetables did not – they still listed only the services between Berwick/Tweedmouth and Kelso!

The public timetables for the summer of 1954 advertised four trains each way between Berwick and St.Boswells. All were specifically marked as through trains but, although none of the westbound trains spent more than 17 minutes at Kelso (the 6.47pm ex-Berwick spent a mere six minutes there – this was positively slick by Tweed Valley standards), three of the four eastbound trains demonstrated the long-standing tradition of giving the passengers ample time to inspect the delights of Kelso station. One of those eastbound trains spent 24 minutes at Kelso and another spent 54 minutes there. By this time there were no Sunday services on the line.

During the early part of the 1950s the motive power situation was very similar to what had gone before: G5 0-4-4Ts from the Tweedmouth end and C15 4-4-2Ts from the St.Boswells end. There were, of course, times when those traditional types were in short supply; for example, due to a shortage of C15s in January 1954 a number of the Tweed Valley passenger trains were worked by J35 0-6-0s. No.64509 of Hawick was noted on Saturday 23 January.

A most unusual visitor to the line in December 1954 was brand-new Standard Class 4 2-6-4T No.80110. The engine had recently been completed at Doncaster Works and was *en route* to its permanent home at Aberdeen. A visit to the area on Tuesday 22 February 1955 found J21 65091 on the 7.15pm passenger train from St.Boswells to Tweedmouth. It was unusual to see a J21 on a passenger working on the line, especially on the 7.15pm ex-St.Boswells as, in the mid-1950s, that train was usually handled by a 'Scott' (D30) 4-4-0.

The summer timetables for 1955 saw a reduction in the already meagre passenger services on the Tweedmouth-Kelso section. Hitherto there had been four passenger trains each way over the entire length of the branch, but that was now reduced to just two, both being worked by a St.Boswells engine. Another economy effected that summer was that, as from Monday 4 July, Velvet Hall, Twizell, Sunilaws, Carham and Sprouston stations all closed to passengers. In contrast, the services on the St.Boswells-Kelso section remained largely unchanged, which meant that Kelso still had four trains to and from St.Boswells.

Yet another economy effected in 1955 was the closure, in August, of the sub-shed at Kelso. Its regular occupant, Sentinel 68138, was transferred to Ayr. Subsequently, shunting at Kelso was performed by the engine of a pick-up goods. This was part of a St.Boswells diagram which started as the 7.19pm St.Boswells-Carlisle (Canal) goods. It left Carlisle at 1.00am and, after returning to St.Boswells, the engine took a pick-up goods to Jedburgh and Kelso. During the late 1950s and early 1960s the engines noted on this job included LMS Crabs, B1s, J37s, J38s and – wait for it – an LMS Jubilee. Yes – a Jubilee on the Tweed Valley line! The engine was 45696 ARETHUSA and the date of its appearance was 29 May 1964.

Going back to the mid-1950s, V3 2-6-2Ts took over some of the St.Boswells-based workings; during the early summer of 1958 Hawick's No.67606 was in regular action on the line. By the late 1950s the V3s had largely been displaced by Standard Class 2 2-6-0s, supplied by Hawick. A visitor to the line on 3 August 1959 (Bank Holiday Monday) noted that No.78049 was returning home with the 4.00pm ex-St.Boswells, the train being formed of just one coach as far as Kelso, where most of the passengers alighted. Two vans of parcels were attached at Kelso (this was a regular practice for the 4.00pm), and the mixed train continued to Berwick. The complement of passengers was just four, and two of those were visiting enthusiasts.

Our visitor on the Bank Holiday Monday added that the Tweed Valley line presented a peculiar contrast as one travelled from the Scottish to the North Eastern Region – the Scottish stations were well tended, but Coldstream (one of the only two North Eastern Region stations which remained open to passengers) was 'in complete and utter contrast with broken fences, no paint and a generally unkempt appearance'.

The following day – 4 August 1959 – a V2 2-6-2 (sadly unidentified) was spotted at Roxburgh on a Hawick-Berwick excursion.

On the operational front there was a small, but nevertheless important, change on 16 November 1959 when St.Boswells shed closed. The engines for the Tweed Valley passenger trains were subsequently supplied direct by Hawick. The use of engines such as the Standard Class 2s – 78046, 78048 or 78049 were the usual ones – on the customary one-coach passenger workings on the Tweed Valley line might seem like a case of over-provision. It is perhaps surprising that diesel railbuses were not introduced on the line in the late 1950s but, that said, *none* of the other Border lines benefit from the attentions of railbuses. Galashiels-Berwick via Tweedmouth could have been an intriguing concept, acting as a feeder to the ECML and using the versatility of a railbus to eradicate the reversal problem at Tweedmouth, but there is no evidence of the authorities even thinking in such terms. Quite the opposite in fact.

The author travelled the line in 1960 – the train was hauled by a V3 – and endured a lengthy wait at Kelso; some such delays were timetabled at 54 minutes. One of the daily services over the length of the line took 130 minutes for 34 miles. In 1961 an unusual burst of enterprise saw an Edinburgh-Kelso evening service introduced – unusually travelling via Peebles, and with a mere five-minute turn-round at Kelso – but this was too little too late.

A return visit to the line in July 1960 found that, because of the local holiday period, the Tweed Valley line was exceptionally busy. Consequently, the branch engine of the day, No.78049, had a hectic time reversing at Tweedmouth and turning at St.Boswells. A steady 55-60mph was maintained between the stations on the double-track between Tweedmouth and Kelso. Our visitor reported there was plenty of freight traffic to be seen in the station yards along the way; J37 64606 of Galashiels was in charge of the branch goods (the diagram of which took in the Jedburgh branch). Other engine classes known to work the goods services on the line at this time are J39 0-6-0s, K3 2-6-0s, B1 4-6-0s and LM-type Ivatt Class 2s.

There was also an intriguing 'might have been'. At some time in the early 1960s a Deltic diesel was tried on the line – after all, these were the successors to the A4s Pacifics which, as we have seen, traversed the line in 1948 – but the Deltic proved to be somewhat less well suited to the task as it knocked over all the ground signals along its route.

The end cometh

The Beeching era proved fatal for the Tweed Valley line. Rail managers on both sides of the Border moved towards closure by publicly advertising the withdrawal of passenger services on 18 June 1963. This was to include the closure of the remaining stations: Maxton, Rutherford (which had been reduced to the status of an unstaffed halt on 2 November 1959), Roxburgh, and Kelso stations on the Scottish side, and Norham, Coldstream, and – surprisingly, perhaps – Tweedmouth, south of the Border.

The posters announcing the closure listed the replacement bus services which were to be operated by Scottish Omnibuses and a smaller company in Kelso, but the replacement buses proved to be a major problem. It soon emerged that the village of Rutherford had no public transport facility on weekdays apart from the trains, and two buses on a Saturday only. It was not enough for BR to point out that *nobody* used the station at Rutherford during a sample of 18 train services in winter and summer. Overall use was scant enough; the total of 18 sampled trains carried only 152 fare-paying passengers – between eight and nine per train. This was borne out by the

Public timetable, 14 June to 19 September 1954

It was customary for the 4.00pm St.Boswells-Berwick to pick up vans from the bay on the north side of Kelso station. On 30 May 1962, this task fell to No.78047. The vans are out of view to the right; once attached at the rear of the solitary coach, 78047 will continue tender-first to Berwick. PHOTOGRAPH: MICHAEL MENSING

fiscal statistics – an outlay annually of £58,920 for a returned income of £2,260.

Public reaction to closure was mixed. Five Scottish-based residents – two of whom were based in Rutherford – objected, but so uninterested were English travellers, that, some ten days before the closing date for objections, the Secretary of the North Eastern TUCC, based in York, suggested to his Edinburgh counterpart that only the Scottish committee need meet, and that English committee members would attend any closure meeting on an informal basis. This highly unusual arrangement appeared in jeopardy when the Borough of Berwick-upon-Tweed formally objected just before the expiry of the deadline. Effectively, Berwick was to lose a main-line station (Tweedmouth); the St.Boswells trains crossing the Royal Border Bridge between Tweedmouth and Berwick were often very well filled, and it was Tweedmouth residents providing the traffic. Interestingly, the borough also cited potential damage to tourism in the area. It seems that this was the only time the word 'tourism' was mentioned in the public debate. Nevertheless, the two TUCCs decided that the Scottish committee would act for both, and a public meeting was announced for Kelso on 11 October 1963.

Archival papers show that the committee travelled to Kelso from Edinburgh by coach hired from Scottish Omnibuses; somewhat perversely, the coach's departure point was Edinburgh Waverley station concourse. At the meeting the officials found that two of the private objectors had failed to attend, but the views of a number of local authorities were heard. An individual who turned up unexpectedly was not allowed to speak as he had failed to lodge an objection within the specified period.

The committee came to the unanimous decision that closure could go ahead, provided a replacement bus service between St.Boswells and Kelso were to include Maxton and Rutherford in its route. Minister of Transport Ernest Marples gave his approval in February 1964. The withdrawal of public passenger services was duly set for Monday 15 June 1964.

The final public timetable for the line showed that the fastest service on the Scottish section was the 6.22am out of St.Boswells which reached Kelso in only 21 minutes despite having to stop at Maxton for the guard to open the level crossing gates. (In 1948 the *Flying Scotsman* had been allowed 26 minutes on the St.Boswells-Kelso section!) The speed of the 6.22am was because the train preserved the tradition of conveying Her Majesty's mails which had been unloaded from the overnight (9.20pm) ex-St.Pancras.

A visitor to the line on Friday 12 June 1964 – just three days before closure – reported that the 4.02pm St.Boswells-Berwick was formed of *three* coaches (two corridors and one non-corridor), but the maximum complement of passengers at any one time was eight, of whom one was a railwayman and three were enthusiasts making a farewell visit. The engine was Hawick's Class 4 2-6-0 No.76050.

In the absence of Sunday services, the last revenue-earning passenger trains ran on Saturday 13 June. The last local service on the line west of Kelso was the 7.33pm running through from Berwick. It was headed by Class 2 No.78048 which, with an uncharacteristic burst of affection, carried a 'Kelso Laddie' headboard.

To replace the trains, two bus services a day were provided, with the BRB subsidising these to the tune of £2,500 (in 1966). A traffic survey conducted in 1967 revealed that 50% of the new services did no business in Rutherford, so permission was requested to withdraw them, despite a petition from 45 villagers (75% of the village's official population). The Minister of Transport (by now Mrs. Barbara Castle) kept them on, but with timetabling changes to encourage increased use. Despite the loss of the passenger services, the line remained open to freight traffic for a little longer. Freight continued between Kelso and Tweedmouth until 1965, the last revenue-earning train being the local goods train on Saturday 27 March. It was worked by Class 3 No.77002 of Tweedmouth shed. That engine had also worked the last Wooler branch goods two days earlier, on 25 March. But this still left the St.Boswells-Kelso section open for goods traffic. However, this officially came to an end on Monday 1 April 1968 when the goods services were formally withdrawn. Latterly they had run on an 'as required' basis, being worked by a Clayton (D8500) diesel from Hawick shed, with a Hawick loco crew and a St.Boswells guard.

Another Standard, another coach, another day... This is 78048 leaving Maxton with the 2.21pm Kelso-St.Boswells on 26 August 1960. The loop clearly hasn't been used for some time – not only are the rails in poor condition, but the signal arm has been removed. PHOTOGRAPH: HUGH BALLANTYNE

Bibliographic note: This article is the result of cross-Border research. Records of the NBR and LNER were researched at the Scottish Record Office, whose staff are thanked for their assistance. TUCC records were also examined. Other YN&B, NER, LNER and BR records, Board of Trade reports and WTTs were sourced at the Public Record Office, Kew. Secondary sources included as Tomlinson's *North Eastern Railway*, an article about the Tweed Valley line in the December 1956 edition of *Trains Illustrated* and various other contemporary magazines, principally the *Railway Observer*. Alan Robinson is thanked for his previously unpublished eye-witness account of the 1948 emergency operations. R.B.Lacey kindly drew our attention to a number of well-researched articles in the *North Eastern Express* (the journal of the North Eastern Railway Association), particularly *The Kelso branch of the NER* by J.C.Dean in issues 71-73 and *Sprouston* by J.F.Addyman in the February 1997 edition. Thanks also to Messrs. Bryan L.Wilson, Bill Lynn, Richard Lacey, Stuart Sellar and Peter Short for invaluable advice and assistance.

Having arrived at St.Boswells with the 9.56am from Berwick, 78049 has run round on the down line and is now preparing to move on to the single coach, which it will then move over to the up side to await departure. The date is 26 May 1962. PHOTOGRAPH: MICHAEL MENSING

FURTHER FINE PHOTOS FROM MR. FORD
All photographs by W.J.Ford; captions by J.Atyeo

One of our very regular photographic contributors for several years has been Mr.W.J.Ford. And we are very grateful to him for that. We have had yet another rummage in the seemingly bottomless box labelled 'Mr.Ford's photos' and a further selection has leapt out at us. We desperately tried to find some common thread linking the pictures – we were even prepared to resort to something embarrassingly cheesy such as 'A Bucketload of Bagnalls', 'Pug Parade in Patricroft' or 'Every Peckett Carries a Government Health Warning' – but there really was no common theme. But what the heck! Do we really need an excuse for grouping together eight rather nice industrial photographs? No we don't! So we hope you find this slice of industrial life as interesting as we do.

We kick off with another embarrassment – *our* embarrassment, that is. It is a splendid picture of work in progress at an ironstone quarry in the 1950s, with a massive stripping shovel (a Ransomes & Rapier?), a typically work-weary industrial saddle tank and a roughly laid railway line, but we're far from certain which quarry it is. Nor can we identify the locomotive – the only clues are that is has outside cylinders, water softening apparatus attached to the smokebox, a pair of chains presumably for working in conjunction with a certain type of tipping wagon and a small-ish nameplate on the tank. Oh dear, oh dear! Nevertheless, we have a sneaking suspicion that this might be either Harlaxton Quarries, about five miles to the west of Grantham, or Colsterworth Quarries, a little to the north of South Witham. The photographer certainly visited both of those quarries – not once, but on several occasions – but as this is just one of literally thousands of pictures he took 40-45 years ago it is hardly surprising that this particular scene escapes immediate identification. So – come on all you industrial buffs. Can anyone enlighten us please? Pretty please??

Another 'ironstone' picture, but this time we know the location. So there! This is the simple but attractive little engine shed on the South Durham Steel & Iron Company's internal railway system at Irchester Quarries, Wellingborough. This isn't a million miles from the home of Rushden & Diamonds Football Club – apologies to any Rushden supporters who are reading this, but your editor-person was in the Cheltenham Town end of the Millennium Stadium on 6th May. But I digress... There was originally a 3ft 8¼in system at Irchester Quarries, but that was replaced by a standard gauge system in 1912; it is thought that this engine shed was built at about that time. The occupant of the shed appears to be Manning Wardle 0-4-0ST No.14 (W/No.1795 of 1912) which was transferred from Wensley Quarries at Preston-under-Soar in North Yorkshire (which were part-owned by the South Durham Steel & Iron Co) in March 1957 and remained at Irchester until August 1969 when it was acquired for preservation by the Quainton Railway Society. It is still at Quainton Road today. The other engine in our picture is one of the Hawthorn Leslie 0-4-0STs, possibly No.15 (W/No.3892 of 1936). The area to the left of the Hawthorn Leslie is a worked-out quarry.

It wasn't only Dai Woodham who stockpiled redundant steam locomotives – queues of discarded steamers could also be found at some industrial sites, though on a somewhat smaller scale than at Barry. Following the introduction of diesel traction at the Port of London Authority's Royal Docks in 1959 the redundant steam locomotives were dumped on various sidings near Custom House shed – this is just one of the sad line-ups which could be seen in early 1960. The queue is formed of Hunslet 'Austerity' 0-6-0STs and Hudswell Clarke 0-6-0Ts; the latter type was synonymous with the Royal Docks – no less than 23 such engines had worked there since 1915, and the majority of those remained in use until the arrival of the first diesels in 1959. This picture was taken looking west – the Royal Victoria Dock is out of view to the left and Custom House shed is behind the photographer to the right. The buildings running more or less left to right in the distance are in Victoria Dock Road, and the footbridge over the railway lines gives access to Custom House station. The Royal Docks closed in 1981 and, of course, the area subsequently underwent a massive transformation.

For anyone who thought that all industrial railways operated in an inhospitably heavy duty environment and involved a liberal helping of muck and grime, perhaps this rustic scene will prompt a rethink. This is the 4ft 3in gauge Broom Bank Railway to the north of Sittingbourne. The railway was used principally to bring clay from pits near the bank of the River Swale, across the open countryside, to the Smeed Dean Cement Works on Milton Creek. It has been opined elsewhere that the railway was built to such an unusual gauge simply because, when the line was laid in 1933, the two second-hand locomotives which were acquired were of that gauge. This is Andrew Barclay 0-4-0ST WOULDHAM (W/No.1679 of 1920) tootling along with a rake of tub wagons between East Hall and the cement works. Delightful!

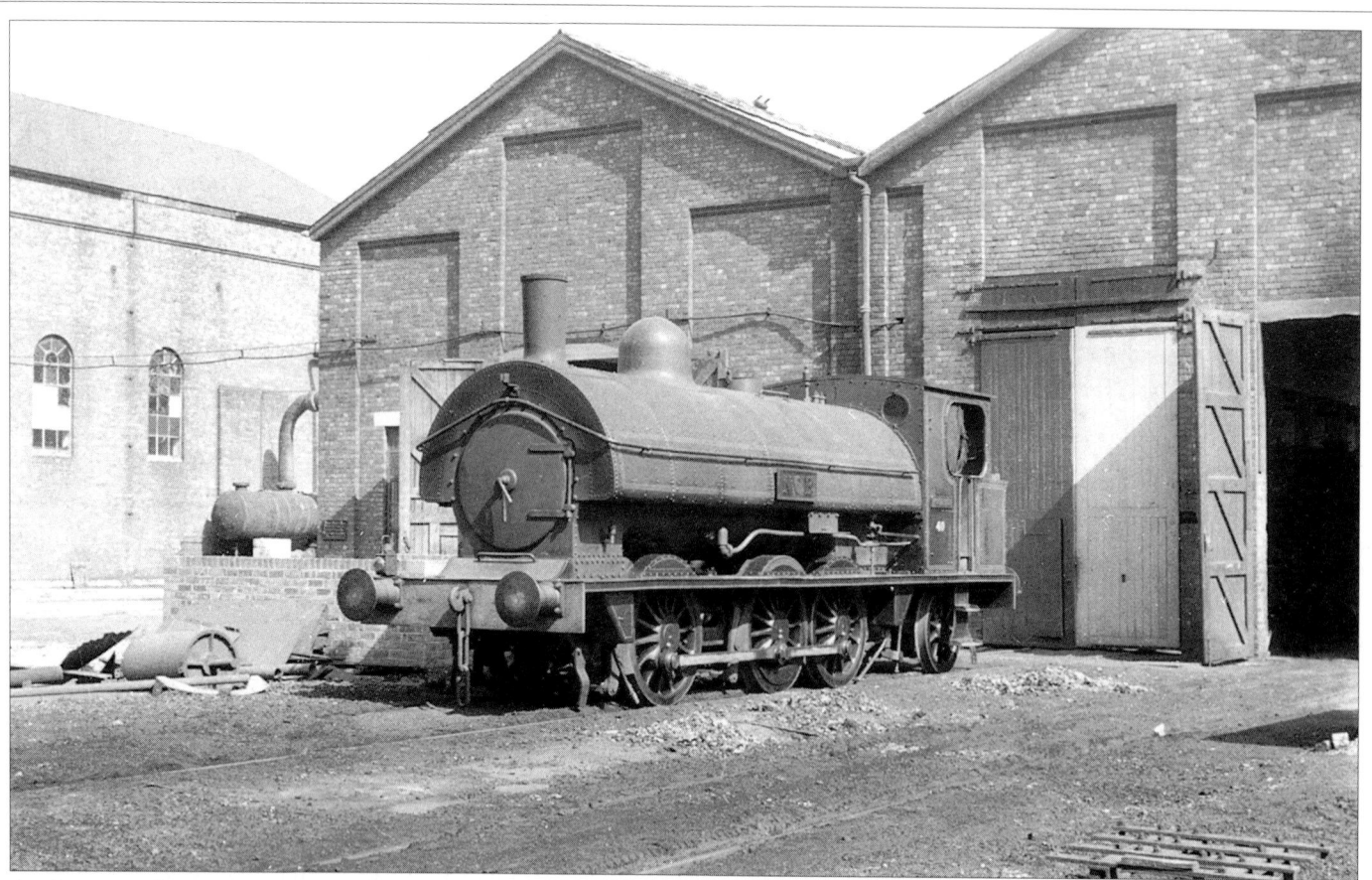

At the more 'heavy duty' end of the industrial scale were collieries. Coppice Colliery near Ilkeston was just one of many hundreds of pits which had their own internal locomotive-worked system, though for industrial locomotive connoisseurs it did have the attraction of four Beyer Peacock engines. Two were purchased second-hand from the Mersey Railway in 1903/04 (one of those was the famous CECIL RAIKES), but the other pair – both 0-6-2STs – were purchased new. For a British colliery company – or any other 'industrial' customer, come to that – to purchase a new Beyer Peacock locomotive was unusual as, although the company was one of the most famous of all Britain's independent locomotive builders, the majority of its locomotives were for 'main line' customers, principally abroad. This picture shows one of Coppice Colliery's rarities – Beyer Peacock W/No.6728, purchased new in 1931 and named WOODSIDE. This handsome creature – which was photographed on 19 April 1953 – certainly fits James Lowe's description of Beyer locomotives: '...good craftsmanship, simplicity and excellence in design and paramount in elegance'. WOODSIDE remained at Coppice Colliery until 1957, when it was scrapped.

Whereas Coppice Colliery's Beyer Peacock might have been the height of elegance and modernity, many industrial locomotives were somewhat less imposing. For example, there was this Hunslet 0-4-0ST (W/No.215 of 1879) which was purchased fourth-hand (at least!) in 1952 by John Varley & Sons for use at their foundries at Atlas Street, St.Helens – it is seen here near Pocket Nook Street, the North Western Gas Board's yard being on the far side of the road crossing. The locomotive had previously worked at Cliffe Hill Granite Quarries in Leicestershire and, before that, it is thought to have been used by the contractor engaged on building a housing estate at Beacontree, Essex. It remained at Varley's until 1960 when it was cut up for scrap.

Returning to the coal industry, the NCB also had its share of antiquities. Or at least, its fair share of antique-*looking* engines. This seemingly ancient Manning Wardle 'F' class 0-4-0ST (W/No.1978) was actually built in 1919; it went new to the East Holywell Coal Co in Northumberland but was acquired by Backworth Collieries in 1932. It was inherited by the NCB in 1947 and was transferred from Backworth to West Wylam Colliery near Prudhoe in 1956. It was photographed at its new home on 6 April 1958, a little over two years before it was unceremoniously scrapped. For the record, it had 10in x 16in cylinders and 2ft 9¾in diameter wheels.

So you wanted real industrial muck and grime? Here's another helping. This is Peckett 'M5' class 0-4-0ST STANLEY, W/No.1314 of 1913, taking on water in the yard of the Wouldham Cement Company, West Thurrock, Essex. The locomotive is in a perfectly presentable condition, but whoever is responsible for the loco yard seems not to be too keen on clearing ash and other debris from the ground. As for the engine itself, it went new to the Wouldham company in 1913 and remained there until being scrapped in 1965.

A FLURRY OF FORECOURTS

The station forecourt might be regarded as a sort of 'welcome-to-our-railway-company' shop window. (Or, these days, as a popular location for the 'where-the-hell-can-I-leave-my-car-for-five-minutes-without-being-charged-an-arm-and-a-leg' challenge.) Our photographs show the 'welcoming' aspect of the station forecourt. This first picture is of Llandrindod Wells station on 2 October 1971. The notice on the left trumpets the seductive offer of a free shopping bag to all passengers on certain day returns. Generous, or what? PHOTOGRAPH: ANDREW MUCKLEY

Moving farther up the Central Wales Line, the station buildings at Knighton looked more like a country house than a place to go and catch a train. Here we have a case of dual nationality. Although the town of Knighton itself is in Wales, only the very tip of Swansea end of the platform is in Wales; the rest of that platform – and, indeed, the rest of the station – is in England. In the distance on the right is the station goods yard; what looks like an 8F is in the yard. This picture was taken on 2 September 1963. PHOTOGRAPH: ANDREW MUCKLEY

On the opposite page we mentioned the present-day problem of parking a car on a station forecourt. Here's a reminder of how things usually were in the late 1950s – oodles and oodles of space and no dire warnings of the charge for releasing wheel clamps. This is Torrington station in North Devon. A marvellous period piece.

Ventnor station on the Isle of Wight was arguably one of the most exquisitely sited stations in Britain, but the passenger entrance and forecourt were, perhaps, a bit of a let-down. Nevertheless, this scene has plenty of interest value, especially for students of Isle of Wight taxis in the early 1960s.

A CONTRACTOR'S JOB

For the construction of the new tunnels at Potters Bar and Hadley Wood, the contractors established their depot near the south end of the original Potters Bar Tunnel. This picture was taken on 11 July 1956 and shows the contractor's sidings with seven of the little Ruston diesels and a number of skips. The flattened strip of ground between the contractor's yard and the BR main line is the alignment on which the two new lines will be laid. In the distance, the south portal of the existing Potters Bar Tunnel can be seen; one can just about make out some construction activity to the left – this will be in connection with the new tunnel. Now, who would have thought that the ECML would ever have found a place in *Bylines*?
PHOTOGRAPH: PHILIP J.KELLEY

When Britain's railways were being built, the contractors often laid their own locomotive-worked railways to help bring materials to the site and to provide a means of transportation between different parts of the site. Quite often, a sizeable fleet of small but sturdy industrial saddle tanks would be engaged; for example, for their contract to construct the GWR/GC joint line from Northolt to High Wycombe in 1901-05, Messrs. Pauling & Co used no less than 33 different locomotives – mostly Manning Wardle or Hunslet 0-6-0STs – at various times. However, by the 1950s very few additions were being made to the country's railway map – indeed, the system was already contracting – so the sight of a major 'railway contractors railway' (a cumbersome description, we'll admit!) was something of a rarity. That said, there was one conspicuous exception. This was the system used by Charles Brand & Son Ltd for building three new tunnels as part of the long-overdue quadrupling of the ECML between Greenwood and Potters Bar. The total length of the new tunnels was 1,830 yards, and it was estimated that some 750,000 tons of earth would have to be excavated and dumped.

For the Potters Bar contract, Charles Brand & Son established their main plant depot near Potters Bar tunnel and laid a 2ft gauge railway which, not only connected the works sites, but also had branches to the concrete factory and the dumping area. For working the railway, a fleet of 28 little Ruston & Hornsby four-wheeled diesel-mechanical locomotives were drafted in; all but four of these were purchased new for the Potters Bar job. The work finally commenced in the autumn of 1955. The May 1956 issue of the *Railway Observer* reported: 'Preparations are well advanced and several hundred Irish labourers are expected in Potters Bar within the next few weeks. Narrow gauge tracks extend from the camp which is to the south of the Great North Road, southwards over the hill under which Potters Bar Tunnel passes, descending after two reversals to the level of the main line at Ganwick, and finishing at the north end of Hadley North Tunnel. A double-track branch diverges to the west just before Hadley North, the lines swinging into the adjoining meadow, apparently for the purpose of depositing tunnel spoil. At the north end of Hadley North and the south of Potters Bar tunnels, permanent cranes have been installed for handling the tunnel segments... The new concrete portal for the north of Hadley North was completed some two weeks ago, and similar works have been going on at the south of Potters Bar. A considerable number of new four-wheeled narrow gauge dumper cars are assembled at the camp and at Ganwick, together with fourteen* Ruston diesel locomotives with side-facing drivers positions. Short trains of only two or three dump cars are apparently envisaged'. (*The figure of fourteen would have been correct at the time the report was written; the other fourteen did not arrive on site until later in 1956.)

A follow-up report appeared in the August 1956 issue of the *RO*: 'At the north end of Potters Bar Tunnel the contractor's railway comes to an end some 100 yards from the portal, at a higher level... Earthworks are virtually complete at both approaches, the cuttings being correctly banked and smoothed off to suit the two extra running lines. The spoil already removed in the course of this work is being tipped on former meadow land midway between the two Hadley Wood tunnels, to the west, utilising the contractor's railway. The portal at the south end of Hadley North Tunnel is being prepared and the fixed crane is in position. There is no access here to the contractor's railway (private property and a public road intervene) unless through the pilot bore. The north end of Hadley South Tunnel will be a difficult site due to the nearness of the road bridge and Hadley Wood Station. The access road is partly made but there is no connection with the contractor's railway... The factory to prepare the concrete tunnel segments is at an advanced stage of completion near the Great North Road. A tall container for dry cement stands at the upper end of the corrugated sheds, which descend in several stages as the processes develop. Parallel narrow gauge tracks run the length of the low-built sheds, emerging from the last level into an open area. A large number of four-wheeled dolly trucks are stockplied here'.

The tunnelling work was completed in early 1959, and the new down slow line – through the new tunnels – was brought into use on 4 April. The first ordinary passenger train to use the new line was a Kings Cross-Hatfield local which left New Barnet shortly after its booked time of 8.43pm. The train's progress through the new tunnels was accompanied by much whistling from the engine; this was partly for the entertainment of the contractors' representatives who were on board, but the other passengers on this ordinary service train were reported to be '…quite bewildered by the brouhaha and totally unaware of the importance of the long-awaited occasion'. The second line through the new tunnels – which meant full four-track operation – was brought into use on 3 May.

The contractor's locomotives returned to the firm's plant depot at Merton. Most were subsequently used on various other contracts, but a few were sold. Two of those which were sold eventually went to the Gin-Gin Co-operative Sugar Milling Association in Australia and another eventually finished up with Bord-na-Mona in Ireland.

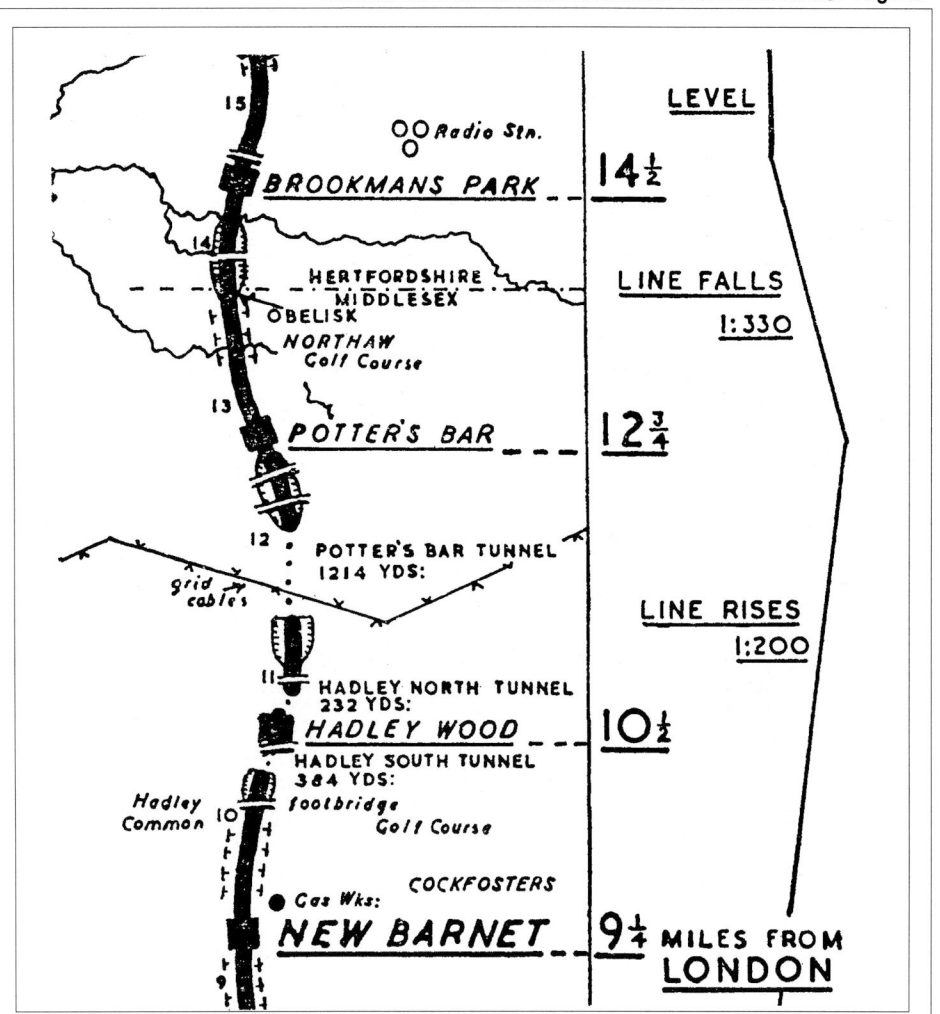

For their 2ft gauge site railway, the contractor's used a fleet of 28 Ruston diesels. All but the four were purchased new specially for the Potters Bar job and were the maker's '48DL' type. That said, there were two types of '48DLs' – this is one of the 7-ton versions fitted with a 4-cylinder '4VRH' engine rated at 44hp. It was photographed at ths south end of Potters Bar depot on 11 July 1956. PHOTOGRAPH: PHILIP J.KELLEY

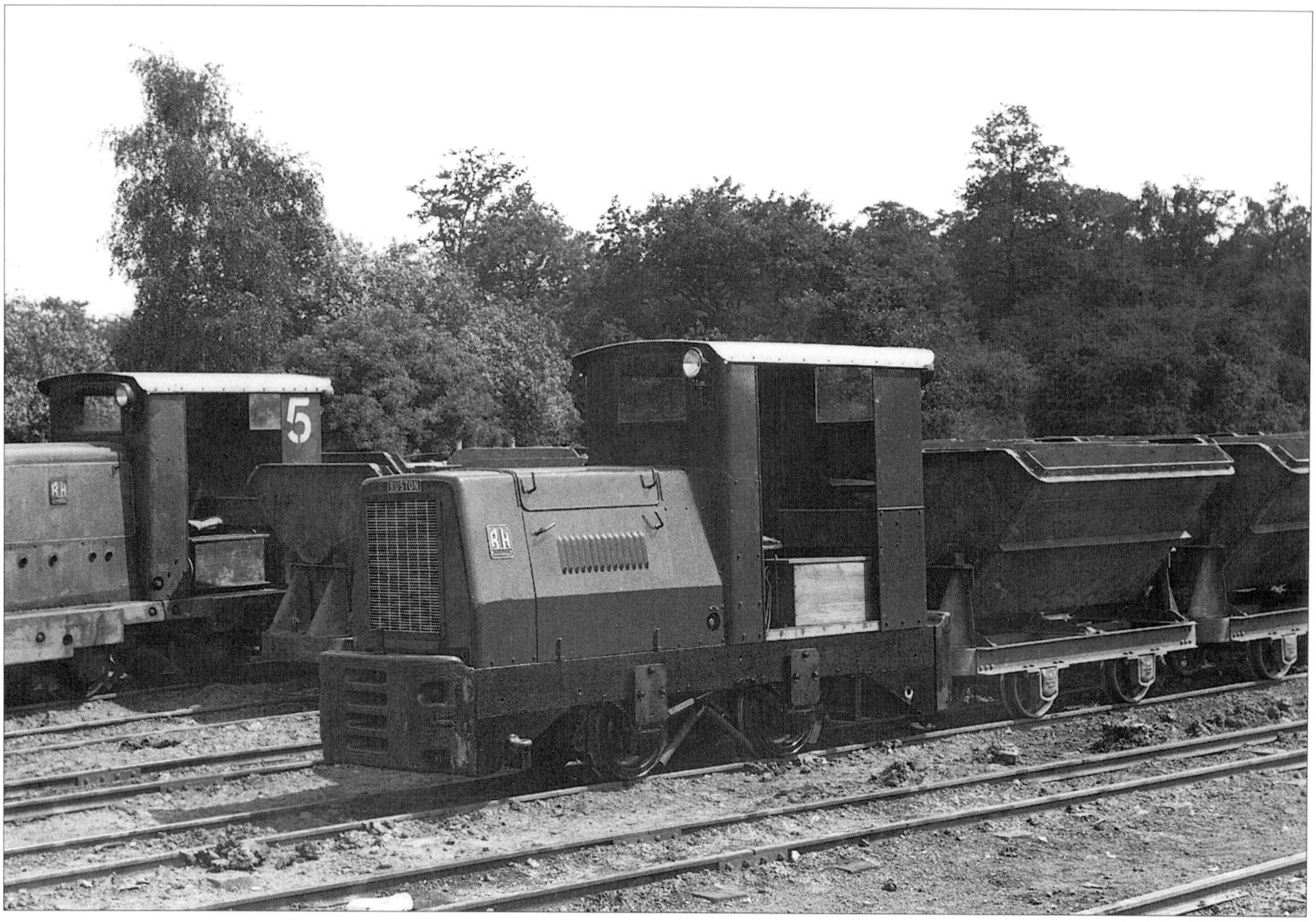
5
RUSTON
RH

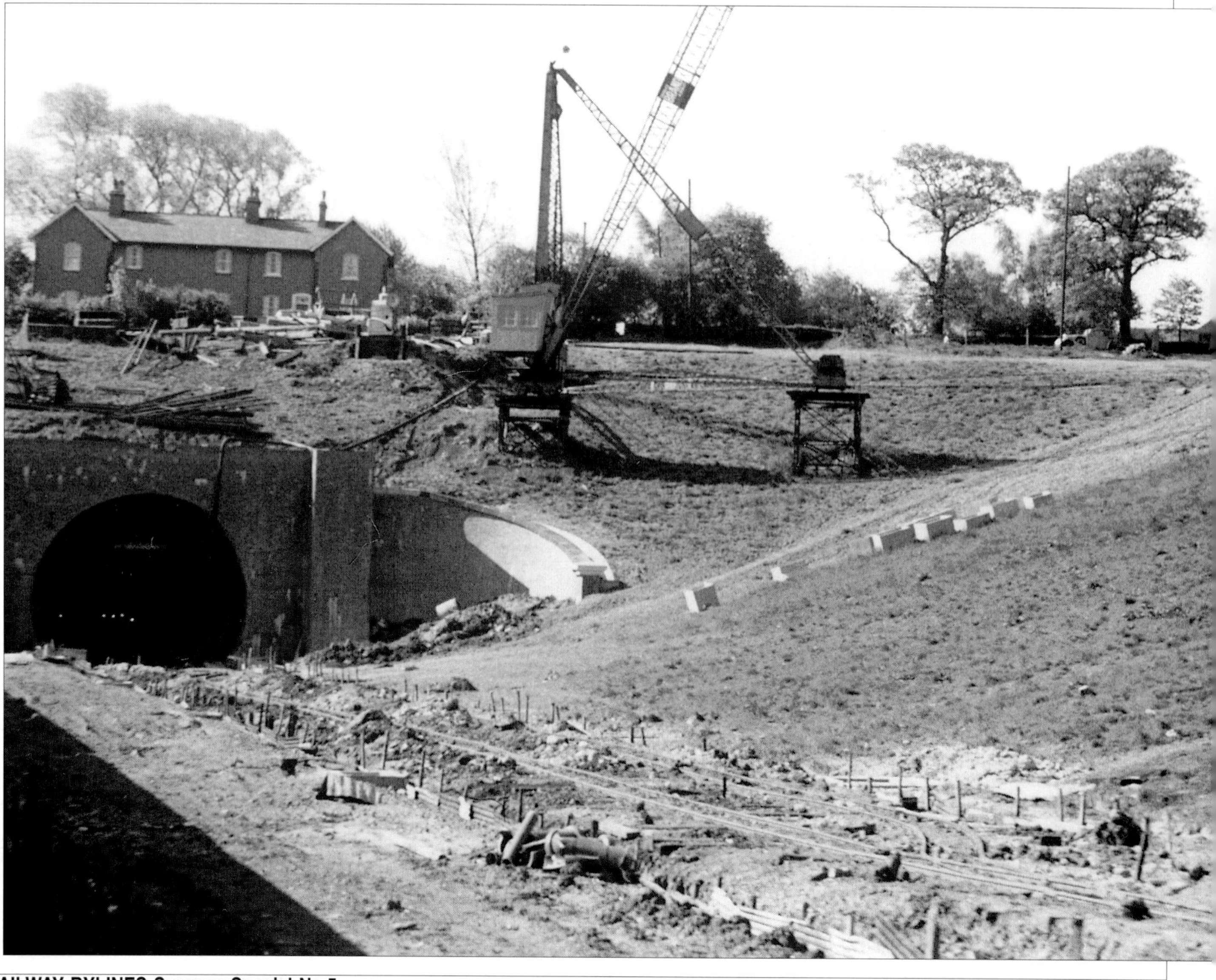

Top left. Two types of Rustons on the contractor's railway at Potters Bar– in the foreground is one of the 5-ton '48DLs' which had a '4YC' engine, while a 7-ton '4VRH'-engined version stands behind. PHOTOGRAPH: PHILIP J.KELLEY

Above. The north end of Potters Bar Tunnel, with one of the fixed cranes which was used to handle the tunnel segments. The report in the August 1956 *Railway Observer* noted that the contractor's railway stopped about 100 yards short of this point, but as far as we are aware it was later extended to the hill above the portal. PHOTOGRAPH: DEREK CLAYTON

Left. This is part of the contractor's site at the north end of Hadley North Tunnel, with the contractor's 2ft gauge railway extending into the recently completed bore. PHOTOGRAPH: DEREK CLAYTON

BARRINGTON CEMENT WORKS AND ITS LIGHT RAILWAY
by Ian P. Peaty

On 14 October 1927 the *Cambridge Chronicle* reported the opening of a cement works by the Eastwood Cement Company near the village of Barrington, some eight miles south-west of Cambridge. This was the final chapter in a saga which had commenced in 1913 when the Dreadnought Cement Company had started constructing a cement works there. An early survey of the two Chalk Marl hills, Chapel Hill and Wilsmere Down, had indicated that there was sufficient high quality material to keep the cement works in business for an estimated two hundred years although, to reach the chalk, some 9,500 tons of top soil would have to be removed. Despite the abundance of reserves the Dreadnought company's project had been shelved in 1914. Although revived in 1916, it had ground to a halt again in 1922 with the works still far from finished.

The enterprise which eventually came to fruition in 1927 was backed by a group of London businessmen, though the controlling interest was held by Eastwoods. At the time of their construction, the works incorporated the world's largest kiln, which had been made by Messrs. Vickers Ltd. The cement works were built close to the hillside, and a small 2ft gauge railway was provided to bring the excavated chalk to a nearby wagon tippler and crushing plant. The crusher had three roads – the two outer tracks were used for tipping the wagons and the middle track looped around an adjacent settling tank. It appears that the 2ft gauge system was brought into use in 1926 (i.e. before the works went into full production), though locomotives were not used until the early 1930s.

In the early 1960s the cement works underwent a major modernisation – the principal aspect was the introduction of a large rotary kiln – and this meant that the demand for chalk virtually doubled. To meet the increased demand a new quarry was opened up about half a mile to the north. It was considered that the 2ft gauge system would be inadequate to cope with the additional 'quarry-to-works' traffic so, when the new quarry became operational in 1963, it was provided with standard gauge lines which were directly connected to the existing Light Railway.

The laying of standard gauge rails to the new quarry in the 1960s rendered most of the old 2ft gauge system redundant, but a section of the narrow gauge was retained between the old quarries and the works until 1976.

Another aspect of the modernisation works of the 1960s was the installation of a new two-road wagon tippler at the quarry. It was built by Strachan & Henshaw of Bristol. The tippler can turn a fully loaded 16-ton wagon through 90° to discharge the raw chalk into the crushing plant. After crushing, the resultant fine chalk passes to two rotary sludge tanks where it is mixed with water and then pumped as a slurry to either a large holding tank (built in 1964) for the rotary kilns, or to the old original open tank for the main works. The slurry is then mixed with gypsum and is calcinated. A by-product of this process is 'rubble' which is used for rail ballast and roadways within the quarry works.

As with the old narrow gauge wagon tippler, the new standard gauge tippler had a through road to help speed up the shunting of wagons.

The track on the new standard gauge quarry lines was short-length 75lb flat-bottomed and spiked rails, but during the winter of 2000 these were replaced by chaired 95lb bullhead rails. The chairs came second-hand – the earliest date

Barrington Cement Works m.p.d., 27 February 1960. This, the old 'engine shed' (we use the term loosely), was located just inside the works site on the north-west side of the Haslingfield Road level crossing, but it was replaced in the 1960s by a smart new shed-cum-workshops a few yards to the west. Here, the engines are, from left to right, Yorkshire Engine Co. W/No.2142, Barclay W/No.919 (in the 'shed') and VULCAN. PHOTOGRAPH: JOHN R.BONSER

and was brought into use in January 1926, being initially used for bringing in materials while the works were under construction. Somewhat logically, the railway was formally titled the Barrington Light Railway; its principal shareholders were Eastwoods Ltd. The Eastwood company's decision to go for a Light Railway Order rather than a conventional – and less-expensive – siding reflected their intention that the line was to be for public use. It was considered that, as the cement works were in a rural location and 1½ miles from the nearest main line station, this could hinder the recruitment of staff, whereas the availability of a passenger-carrying railway direct to the works would make employment there a rather more attractive proposition. The Light Railway Order even stipulated minimum fares of one penny per journey in either direction, and also there was a scale of charges for parcel traffic. However, it is apparent that neither of these services was ever implemented as, when the line eventually opened, the country was in the grip of a recession and workers were usually only too willing to take what ever jobs were on offer, no matter how they would have to

found by this writer is 1925, while several other chairs are dated between 1937 and 1945 and are of LMS origin. As can be seen on the accompanying plan, the quarry lines incorporate a tightly-curved triangular formation terminating in a headshunt. One thing that the plan can not show is that this part of the system is in a delightfully sylvan setting. The headshunt part of the triangle terminates with a 'rail and timber' buffer stop which has a cast iron plate indicating that this part of the track was installed by Thos. W.Ward Ltd of Albion Works, Sheffield.

In 1962 – while the modernisation work was in progress – the old Eastwoods Cement Company became part of the mighty Rugby Portland Cement Company. The premises are still part of the Rugby empire today.

The Light Railway

Going back to the very early days of the cement works in the 1920s, an integral part of Eastwood's operations was a standard gauge rail connection between the works and a point near Foxton station on the LNER's Cambridge-Hitchin line. This connection – a 1½-mile line – was authorised and built as a Light Railway

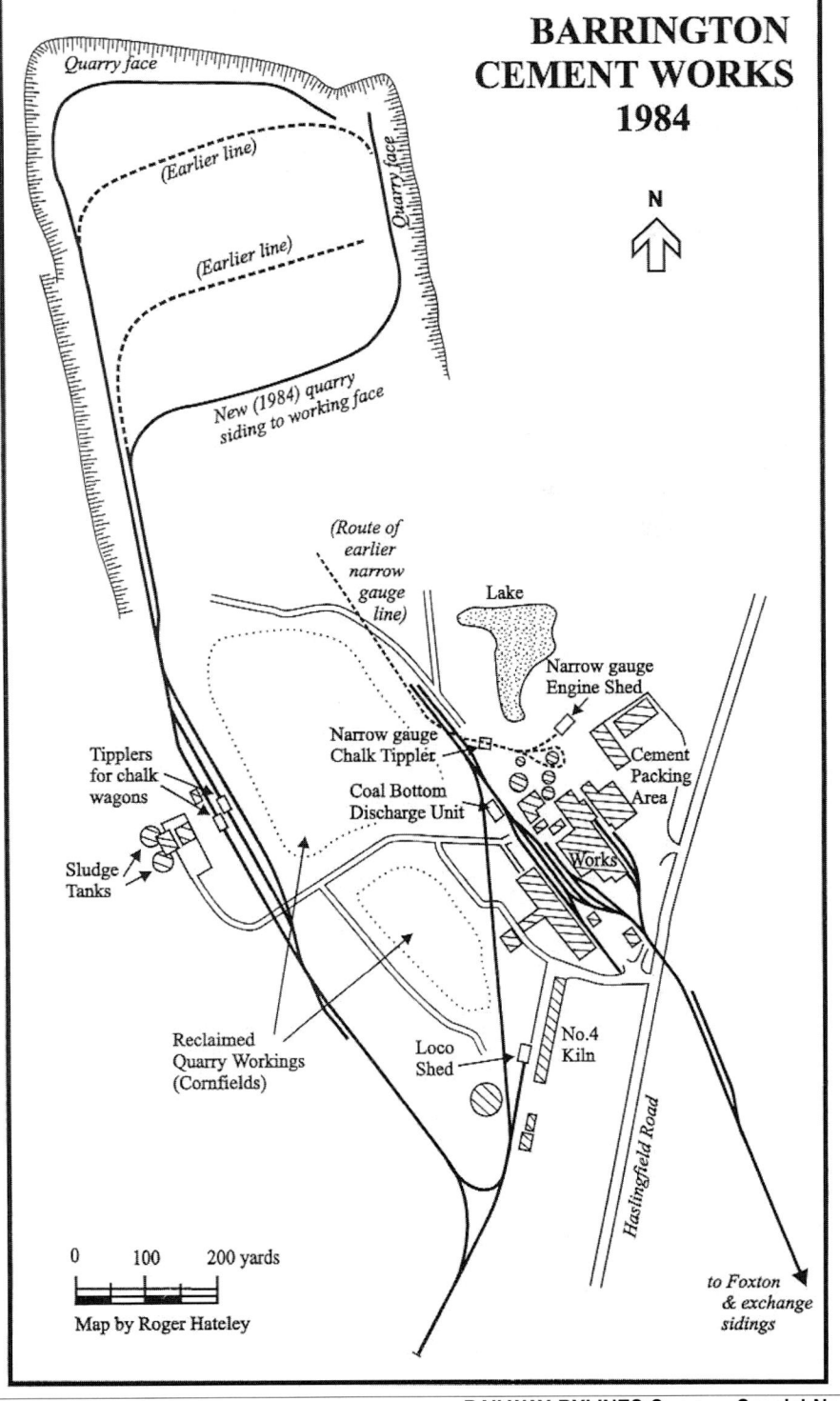

The splendid little Barclay 0-4-0ST VULCAN spent 34 years at the Barrington works. In this mid-1950s picture, the rear buffer-less engine is propelling a rake of wagons past the company offices which were on the north-west side of Haslingfield Road. These offices have since been superseded by a more modern flat-roofed building. PHOTOGRAPH: W.J.FORD

get to their place of employment. An interesting aspect of the original Light Railway Order was that it specified electricity as an alternative to steam power. This is thought to be because Eastwood's had experience of this form of traction at their Lower Halstow brickworks on the Medway estuary where, as early as 1902, a 'trolley pole' locomotive built by A.Hirst & Son of Dewsbury had been introduced on the 2ft gauge line.

Looking at the Barrington Light Railway today, the single-track line diverges from the main line on a 6-chain curve which turns almost 90° in a northerly direction and splits into three exchange sidings which, over several years recently, have been extended as far as possible up to the level crossing over the Foxton Road. Three double slip crossovers were installed in the early 1980s to provide greater flexibility. Northwards from the exchange sidings the Light Railway rises on gradients of 1 in 177, 1 in 115 and 1 in 139 to cross the River Cam by means of a 235-yard-long ferro-concrete viaduct consisting of eight flat arches. From the north end of the viaduct the line keeps rising and, a short distance before the cement works, there is a level crossing over Haslingfield Road (which provides the road access into the works). On the south side of the crossing is a single siding which was used for the storage of cement wagons – either 'Presflos' or 'Procors' – which had been filled during the night shift. On the entire length of the Light Railway, it is stipulated that the weight of locomotives should not exceed 12 tons and that the maximum speed is 25 miles per hour.

When the author last visited the site in July 1986 the single track immediately split into a 'Y' junction after entering the cement works; the right-hand fork served three sidings into the cement packing areas while the left-hand line divided into multiple sidings and loops which served the main part of the works. These came together at the northern end nearest the quarry, with a double headshunt on which was situated the coal discharge plant, now used by Merry-Go-Round (MGR) trains. From one of these two headshunts a line diverged on a downward grade to the locomotive shed and workshops, and then connected with the quarry railway.

The railway at work

As about 8cwt of coal is consumed during the production of one ton of cement, it follows that the principal inwards traffic at Barrington is coal.   Until the mid-1980s the inward coal traffic averaged 2,000 tons per week and arrived in 16-ton mineral wagons. The coal is a fine pulverised slack which is combined with crushed gypsum, about 300-350 tons of which also came in by rail each week. At peak times as many as seventy loaded 16-ton coal wagons arrived at the exchange sidings in a day, and this required the then solitary 'Light Railway' locomotive to make as many as six or seven journeys to the works per day. Another aspect of the inward rail traffic up to the 1980s was spare parts for the plant and machinery. At that time train working normally began at around 6.00am and continued until the line closed at 5.00pm. In steam days the duties of driver and fireman were combined, the second member of the engine crew acting as level-crossing keeper, point-changer and wagon coupler.

During the latter part of the 1980s coal was brought into the works using bottom-discharge MGR wagons. One train of loaded wagons was brought in to the exchange sidings at 11.00am and there was another train in the afternoon, the BR locomotive, usually a Class 47, pushing its consignment into one of the two outer roads of the exchange sidings. Here the wagons were divided to be taken to the works; at this time this usually involved three trips per day with 12 wagons per trip.

As for outward rail traffic, somewhat predictably this used to consist mainly of cement. That said, rail-borne cement traffic ceased in 2000. In earlier times bagged cement had been conveyed in sacks in 12-ton 'Shocvans', but by the mid-1970s that business had been taken over by road transport. By the early 1980s most of the cement was dispatched in bulk. As the manufacture of cement is a continuous process, the output of the night shift at the works was stored in vertical silos which discharged by gravity into sealed 20-ton 'Presflo' wagons. After loading, these wagons were then taken to the single siding just across Haslingfield Road level crossing where they waited to be taken down to Foxton at 10.15am the following morning. Empty cement wagons were then collected from the exchange sidings on an 'as required' basis ready for loading at the works during the day. The 'Presflos', incidentally, were rather ungainly wagons with numerous external ribs and were painted in a bauxite colour. On reaching their destination they were unloaded by forcing compressed air into the sealed tank.

The 'Presflos' were replaced in the mid-1980s by modern silver-liveried 'Procor' tank wagons. Two types of 'Procors' were used. One had 55 tonnes capacity and was built of stainless steel and lined with enamel, with top access by means of double steps at one end. The other type was a 51-tonne powder wagon which had a payload of 38.3 tonnes; this type incorporated a tank with a pronounced dip in the centre which facilitated the flow of powder into the bottom discharge.

The powerful-looking Yorkshire Engine Co 0-6-0ST (W/No.2142 of 1927) stands in the engine shed yard on 27 February 1960. Its livery is black with yellow lettering and red rods. Various bits of debris including old gear wheels, scrap metal and even a spoke-wheeled platelayers trolley lie abandoned. PHOTOGRAPH: JOHN R.BONSER

These 51-tonne wagons were built by BR Engineering at Ashford and were hired out by Tiger Railcar Leasing (UK) Ltd, a subsidiary of an American company, to major UK cement producers. The minimum curve that these four-wheeled tanks can traverse is only 3 chains, although there were no tight curves at the Barrington Cement Works.

When the 'Presflo' wagons were in use up to twenty per day were dispatched, but with the larger 'Procor' wagons only eight per day were sent out. The destinations were the Rugby Portland Cement depots at Bow (London), Tilbury (Essex) and Norwich.

To marshal coal or cement wagons at the exchange sidings, the Barrington locomotives used the 6-chain curve as a headshunt. This allowed for up to eleven or twelve wagons plus the tandem

VULCAN in the shed yard on 2 June 1952. Not only do we see another accumulation of scrap metal and other debris, but the remains of the wooden sleepers in the foreground indicate the alignment of an old siding. PHOTOGRAPH: JOHN R.BONSER

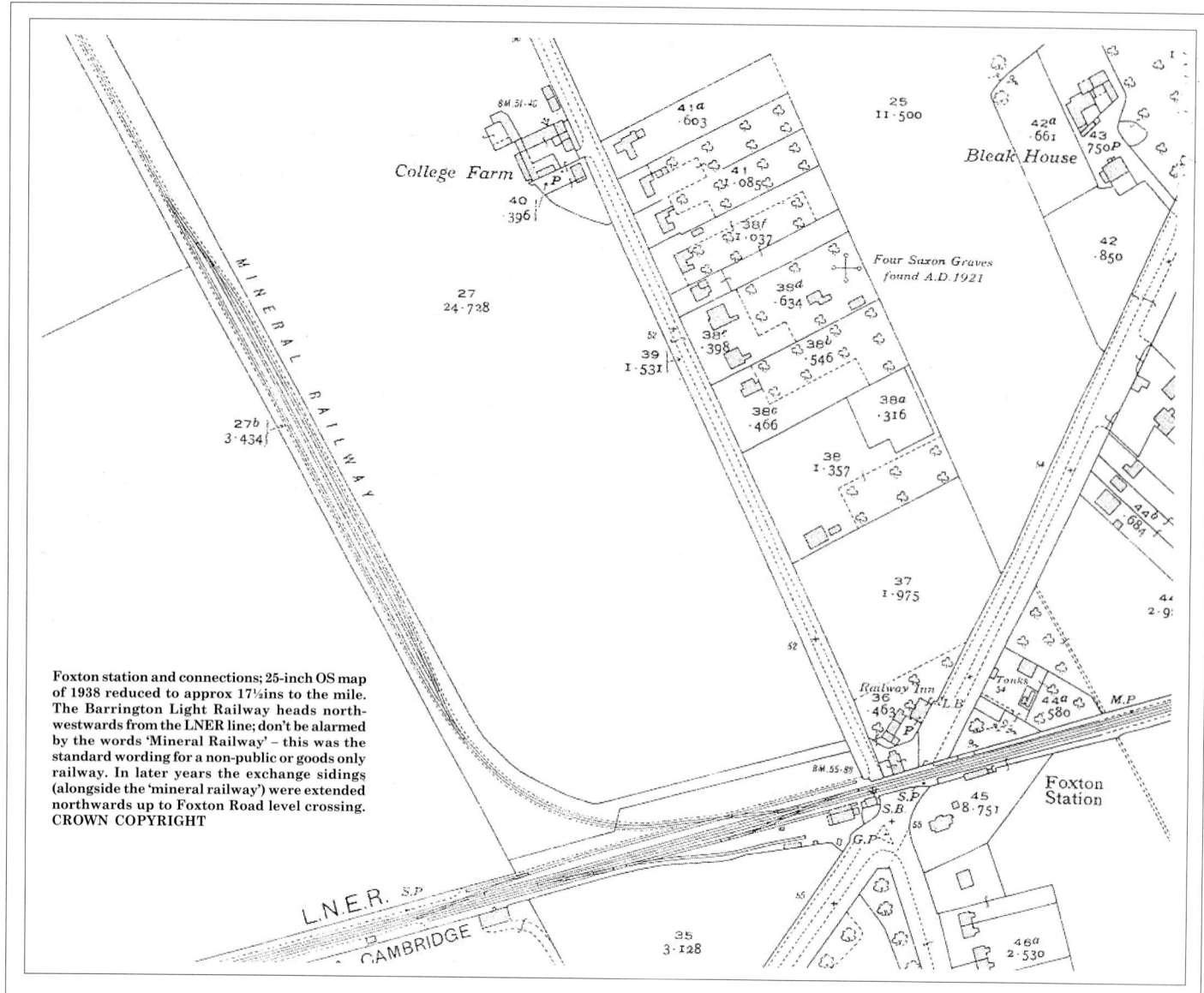

Foxton station and connections; 25-inch OS map of 1938 reduced to approx 17½ins to the mile. The Barrington Light Railway heads north-westwards from the LNER line; don't be alarmed by the words 'Mineral Railway' – this was the standard wording for a non-public or goods only railway. In later years the exchange sidings (alongside the 'mineral railway') were extended northwards up to Foxton Road level crossing. CROWN COPYRIGHT

Sentinels to proceed up to an electronic warning beam which marks the boundary of the private railway. The train could then reverse back to the exchange sidings and connect up to a brake van which had been brought in by the BR locomotive and positioned on one of the outer roads. As soon as the Barrington locomotives had uncoupled and ran up through the central siding, the BR diesel ran forward over the neck of the exchange siding and reversed on to the made-up train which comprised either empty coal wagons or, in earlier times, full cement wagons.

Because the Light Railway is on a downhill gradient towards Foxton, as a safety precaution the locomotives are always at the Foxton end – i.e. the 'downhill' end – of the trains, even though this means propelling from Foxton to the cement works.

At the quarry

In the days of narrow gauge operations at the original quarry, the wagons were the ubiquitous four-wheeled Hudson steel-bodied side tipplers. But now, with only the standard gauge in operation, the fleet comprises 48 wagons, all of 16-ton capacity and built by the Standard Wagon Company. Many date to the 1920s. The livery is light grey with the exception of numbers 1, 2, 3 and 4 which are duck-egg green; many are still inscribed with the title 'Eastwoods Ltd'. The solebars and wheels are black; most have double-spoked wheels.

Track re-alignments are constantly made by a gang of four or five men who are able to either slew the rails or to lay a new track, as only short length rails are used in the quarry. To work the two quarry faces there is a Ruston Bucyrus face shovel and a drag line which has an 80ft boom; both load chalk directly into the internal user wagons.

At the quarry itself, two locomotives are usually in use at any given time. Loaded wagons are propelled in rakes of seven or eight down the gradient to one or other of the tracks at the tippler, where the wagon brakes are applied. The tippler operator unhooks one wagon at a time, eases the brake and allows the wagon to roll forward by gravity, and by holding a catch point lever he is able to direct the wagon into the covered tippler bay. The wagon brake is then applied fully. Any empty wagons occupying the road are slowly pushed forward and out of the tippler. Each successive wagon pushes the previous empty one farther along the siding, and the empties are then coupled together. After the quarry engine has uncoupled from its train it runs round the full length of the tippler sidings via the passing loop; it stops opposite the tippler, and one of the two enginemen releases the brakes of the empty wagons so that they can be gravitated down the gradient to a short spur. The engine then picks these empties and takes them back, via the passing loop at the tippler, to the quarry for a repeat operation.

Barrington locomotives

From 1927 until 1954 there were no more than two standard gauge locomotives at Barrington at any given time. The first to arrive was Andrew Barclay 0-4-0ST VULCAN (W/No.1145 of 1909) which had previously worked at the Ministry of Munitions projectile factory at Lancaster. The next was Peckett W4 class 0-4-0ST LIGHTMOOR (W/No.906) which had been built in 1902 for Henry Crawshay & Co of Cinderford, but was purchased by Eastwoods from Henry Boot Ltd, the contractors engaged on building the Barrington Light Railway.

LIGHTMOOR was transferred to Eastwoods works at Kempston Hardwick, Bedfordshire, circa 1930, but in 1933 Andrew Barclay 0-4-0ST (W/No.919 of 1902) made the opposite journey, being transferred from Kempston Hardwick to Barrington. The two Barclays soldiered on on their own at Barrington – in fact, VULCAN had a couple of years totally on its own in the mid-1940s while W/No.919 had a stint back at Kempston Hardwick – until 1954 when a Yorkshire Engine Co 0-6-0ST (W/No.2142 of 1927) was purchased from the Appleby Frodingham Steel Company. The Yorkshire 0-6-0ST

Barclay W/No.919, showing off its substantial dumb buffers in the 'engine shed' on 27 January 1960. PHOTOGRAPH: JOHN R.BONSER

was painted black with the name EASTWOODS in yellow lettering, whereas VULCAN and LIGHTMOOR had been painted green with the letters 'B L R' in gold.

There were no further changes to the locomotive fleet until 1960 when an RSH 0-4-0 diesel-mechanical was purchased new. This locomotive was powered by a 6L3 Gardner engine rated to develop 153hp at 1,200rpm, giving a maximum speed of 13.8mph. In 1961 the two Barclays were laid aside (they were cut up on site later that year), their eventual replacement being a second-hand Barclay 0-6-0 diesel-mechanical which had formerly been owned by ICI and used at Grangeston, Ayrshire.

The modernisation of 1963 – the opening of the new quarry and the extension of the standard gauge system – meant that additional locomotives were required. To meet this need, two new Ruston & Hornsby '165DE' Class 0-4-0 diesel-electrics were purchased in 1963; these took over most of the work on the quarry lines.

The arrival of the two Rustons did not signal a complete and irreversible switch to diesel power as, in 1965, three 100hp Sentinel steam locomotives and an Avonside 0-4-0ST (W/No.1875 of 1921) were transferred to Barrington from the Rugby Cement works at Totternhoe in Bedfordshire where rail working had recently ceased. The Sentinels remained at Barrington only until 1967 when they were sold to Thomas Hill; their replacements were a new Thomas Hill diesel-hydraulic and a Hibberd diesel which had latterly worked for J.Lyons & Co at their Greenford factory. The Hibberd diesel was, however, found to be underpowered for the Light Railway so it was used instead as the works shunter.

These changes to the locomotive fleet meant that Avonside W/No.1875 was now the only steamer left on site, though its usual role was as the spare engine. It remained on site until 1972 when it was acquired for preservation. All later additions to the Barrington fleet were diesels; some were transferred from other cement works, but others were purchased second-hand. In the 1970s and 1980s all the purchases were made via Thomas Hill of Kilnhurst.

Among the second-hand purchases was a Rolls-Royce powered six-wheeled 'Steelman' (W/No.10275 of 1969) which was acquired in 1982, principally to deal with the air-braked bottom-discharge coal wagons at the newly installed plant. However, the 'Steelman' had a rather short life at Barrington, its heavy axle loading being considered potentially damaging to the River Cam viaduct. It was therefore sent to Rugby Cement's Halling Works at Rochester, Kent; in exchange a pair of their Sentinel diesels, W/Nos.10035 and 10040, came to Barrington in April 1983. These two, which became Nos.R13 and R14, had been adapted by Thomas Hill at Kilnhurst (prior to being sent to Rochester) to work in tandem. They continue to do so today, thus overcoming the viaduct problem.

In their days at Rochester the pair of 'tandem' Sentinels had been painted in a bright orange livery with yellow and black footsteps at each end and similar coloured chevrons to their buffer beams; the handrails had also been painted yellow. However, in 1983 this startling livery was replaced by a more elegant Brunswick green which, by this time, had become the standard livery at Barrington. The green livery is unlined, but the front and rear buffer beams have yellow and black chevrons while the wheels rims are painted white. Another of the diesels – No.15, which had been rebuilt by Thomas Hill in 1972 – sports a deep skirting to the full length of its footplate; this is also painted in chevrons. Although the locomotives working in the quarry get liberally coated with white chalk dust, those used on the Light Railway are kept in a very good cosmetic condition.

To return to the locomotives themselves, the other comings and goings at Barrington in the last twenty years have included Rolls-Royce W/No.10260, a 4-wheeled diesel-hydraulic, which came to Barrington in 1983. It had been built

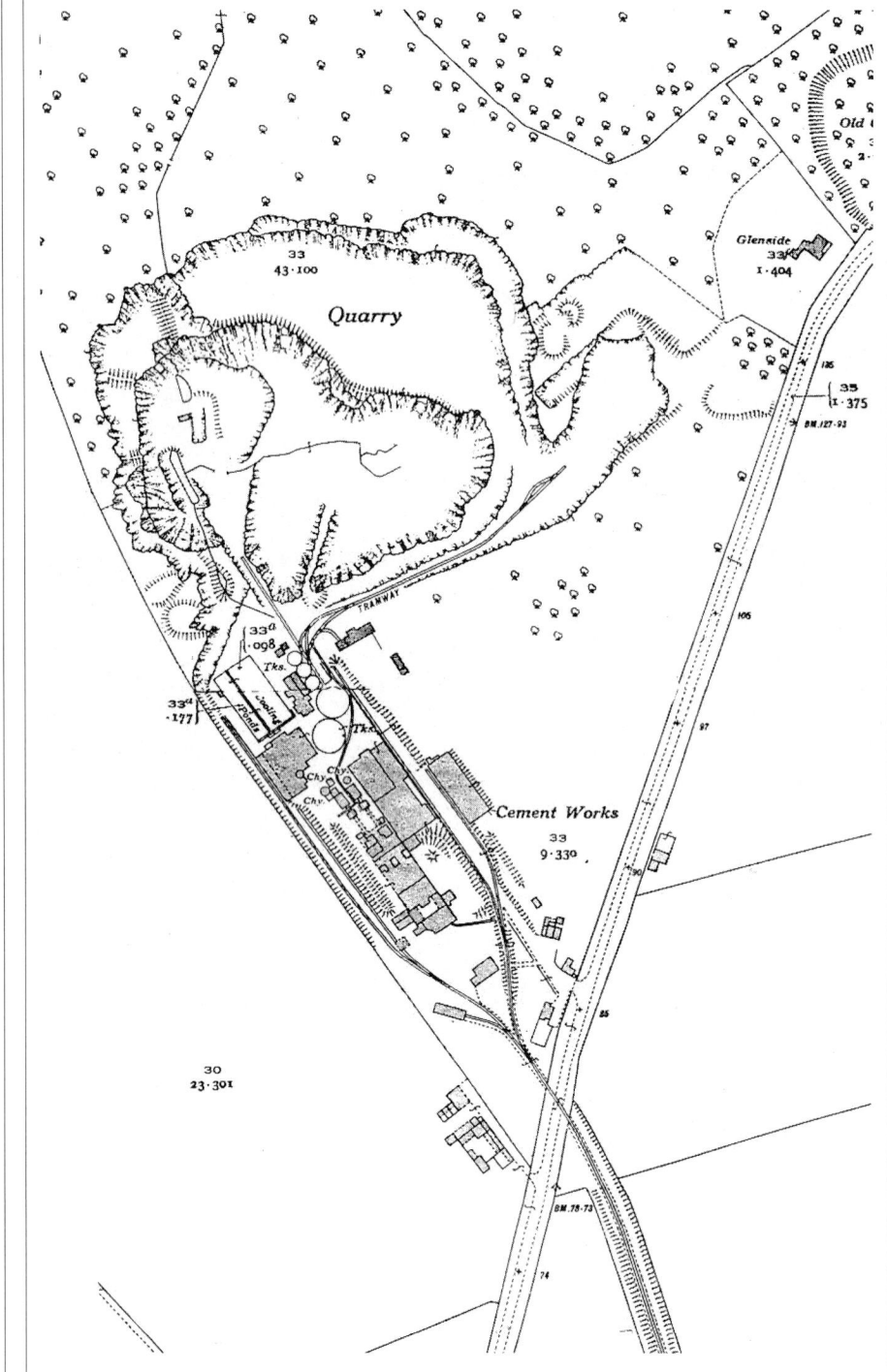

This 25-inch OS map (also reduced to approx 17½ins to the mile) is dated 1926. At this time Eastwoods were still in the process of constructing the works, but it is evident that the 2ft gauge tramway was already laid. The road running vaguely north-south past the works is Haslingfield Road; some of our photographs were taken from the vicinity of the level crossing. CROWN COPYRIGHT

Narrow gauge locos

During the fifty or so-year life of the 2ft gauge system at the old quarries and latterly at the cement works, a total of twelve different locomotives were used. The first ones were very small four-wheeled diesels – two were built by the German firm of Orenstein & Koppel and the other was built by F.C.Hibberd of Park Royal. In 1940 a Kerr Stuart 'Tattoo' class 0-4-2ST was purchased second-hand from the Hunslet Engine Co. This little locomotive had been built in 1915 for the War Office but had latterly been owned by the Durham County Water Board and used during the construction of Burnhope Reservoir near Wearhead. After the reservoir was completed the 0-4-2ST – along with several of the other locomotives which had been employed there – was purchased by Hunslet for resale. This characterful veteran was scrapped at Barrington *circa* 1958, though it had not performed any work for several years previously and had become almost derelict.

Over the years the quarry workings extended farther and farther into the hillside and the distance between the operational faces and the cement works increased accordingly. This placed an ever-growing strain on the locomotive fleet which, for many years, had comprised only four lightweight machines. It was realised that more-powerful locomotives were required and so, in May 1951, a new 6-ton 32/42hp Motor Rail diesel was purchased. Two identical locomotives were acquired second-hand from the Marston Valley Brick Company of Ridgmont, Bedfordshire, a year later. The new additions to the fleet enabled two of the older locomotives to be laid aside. They were eventually scrapped.

The Barrington fleet was augmented by further Motor Rail diesels – two 32/42hp versions and three 50hp versions, all purchased new – between 1954 and 1961. Thus, by 1961 the Barrington company had a total of six fairly modern Motor Rails for use at the quarry; this enabled two of the older ones (the pair which had been purchased second-hand in 1952) to be transferred to lighter duties at Eastwood's works at South Ferriby in Lincolnshire.

As we have seen, the new quarry which was opened up in the 1960s was laid with standard gauge rails. Although this rendered most of the old 2ft gauge system redundant (several of the locomotives were transferred to the Rugby Cement factories at Egham and South Ferriby), a short section of the narrow gauge was retained between the old quarries and the works. Three of the Motor Rails were kept for this section. However, this last bit of 2ft gauge remained in use only until 1976. By this time two of the three remaining Motor Rails had also been transferred to South Ferriby; the third was sold in August 1976 to M.E.Engineering of Cricklewood. That said, the remains of one of the old Orenstein & Koppel diesels (W/No.3444 of 1930) were still on site, despite the fact that that locomotive had been reported derelict as long ago as 1953(!). The remains were later acquired

in 1966 and had been sent new to the APCM's Kent Works; it had later been used by Thomas Hill as a hire loco, but was purchased by the Rugby Group in 1983 for use at Barrington. More recently, a 179hp Thomas Hill diesel was transferred to Barrington from the Rugby Cement works at Chinnor in 1990 and, later that year, a Ruston & Hornsby 0-4-0 diesel-electric was purchased from the Yorkshire Water Authority; it had latterly worked at Blackburn Meadows sewage works at Sheffield. In 1998 Ruston & Hornsby 4-wheeled diesel ELIZABETH was acquired from T.J.Thompson of Millfield Scrapyard, Stockton-on-Tees, and in July 2000 another 4-wheeled Ruston (No.9) arrived from Staffordshire Locomotives. The most recent arrivals (at the time of writing – April 2002) have been a Thomas Hill four-wheeled diesel-hydraulic which came from Rochester Works in June 2001 and a GECT six-wheeled diesel which came from Lindsey Oil Refinery in November 2001.

Prior to the modernisation of the 1960s the standard gauge engine shed – a corrugated iron structure which had long since lost most of its panels – was near the cement works, just on the north-west side of the Haslingfield Road level crossing. However, it was replaced by a new single-road shed on a spur off the 'triangle' a little to the south of the cement works. Adjacent to the new shed was an engineering workshop which carries out repairs to locomotives and internal user wagons as well as plant and machinery.

VULCAN stands with a rake of mixed wagons – wooden- and steel-bodied – near the gangers' shed at the exchange sidings in the 1950s. The BR line is behind the photographer. The lightweight nature of the rails is evident. Note also the timber 'barriers' across two of the three sidings; the timbers appear to be fitted with a lifting handle at one end and a spike at the other, which suggests that they were intended to be swung clear of the siding as required. One imagines that they were intended as a form of moveable 'do not proceed past this point' markers but, given that the engine would have had to proceed (past the photographer) in order to run round, one wonders quite how the system worked. PHOTOGRAPH: W.J.FORD

by Mr.Peter Briddon of Sheffield who is intending to restore the locomotive.

The narrow gauge engine shed was at the north end of the cement works.

Return to steam
On 23 and 26 June 1996 there was a return to steam working at Barrington. This was the result of an agreement between the Rugby Cement company, the Industrial Railway Society and the Rutland Railway Museum, two of the museum's preserved locomotives being used at the quarries for the two days. The locomotives were Avonside 0-4-0ST DORA

Official records show that Barrington's 2ft gauge Kerr Stuart 'Tattoo' class was scrapped in 1958, but this picture of it was taken in 1949 and, quite clearly, the engine was already in an advanced state of dereliction, some of which seems to have been deliberately inflicted.
PHOTOGRAPH: FRANK JONES

BARRINGTON LIGHT RAILWAY and CEMENT WORKS – summary of locomotives

Listed in order of acquisition
Details taken from *Industrial Locomotives of East Anglia* (published by the Industrial Railway Society, 1993) and subsequent update lists
Makers abbreviated thus: AB – Andrew Barclay; **AE** – Avonside Engine Co; **FH** – F.C.Hibberd; **GECT** – GEC Traction; **KS** – Kerr Stuart; **MR** – Motor Rail; **OK** – Orenstein & Koppel; **P** – Peckett; **RH** – Ruston & Hornsby; **RR** – Rolls Royce; **RSH** – Robert Stephenson & Hawthorns; **S** – Sentinel; **TH** – Thomas Hill; **YE** – Yorkshire Engine Co

(a) standard gauge

Name/No.	Type	Maker; W/No.	Wheels	Cyls/h.p.	Built	Acquired	Disposal
VULCAN	0-4-0ST	AB; 1145	3' 5"	14" x 22" (o)	1909	1927 ex-MoM	5.1961; scrapped on site
LIGHTMOOR	0-4-0ST	P; 906	3' 2"	14" x 20" (o)	1902	1928 ex-contractor	c.1930 to Kempston Hardwick
-	0-4-0ST	AB; 919	3' 0"	10" x 18" (o)	1902	1933 ex-Kempston Hardwick ¶	5.1961; scrapped on site
-	0-6-0ST	YE; 2142	3' 4"	15" x 22" (o)	1927	10.1954 ex-Appleby Frodingham Steel Co	3.1965 Scrapped
-	0-4-0DM	RSH; 7924	3' 3"	153hp	1959	New	6.1962 to Eastwoods, Lewes (P)
-	0-6-0DM	AB; 364	3' 6"	180hp	1943	12.1961 ex-Andrew Barclay	c.4.1965; scrapped
7	0-4-0DE	RH; 499435	3' 2½"	165hp	1963	New	-
8	0-4-0DE	RH; 499436	3' 2½"	165hp	1963	New	(out of use by 11.2000)
2	0-4-0ST	AE; 1875	2' 11"	12" x 18" (o)	1921	2.1965 ex-RPC Totternhoe	c.9.1972 (P)
No.11	4w VBT	S; 9564	2' 6"	100hp	1954	4.1965 ex-RPC Totternhoe	c.10.1967 to Thomas Hill
No.12	4w VBT	S; 9565	2' 6"	100hp	1954	4.1965 ex-RPC Totternhoe	c.10.1967 to Thomas Hill
No.13	4w VBT	S; 9556	2' 6"	100hp	1953	4.1965 ex-RPC Totternhoe	c.7.1967 to Thomas Hill
9	4w DH	TH; 186v	3' 2"	210hp	1967	New	4.1983 to Blue Circle, Holborough; Returned 6.2001 ex-Rochester Works
14	4w DM	FH; 3716	3' 1½"	77hp	1955	5.1967 ex-J.Lyons	6.1983 to Thomas Hill
15	4w DH	TH; 240v‡	2' 8"	178hp	1972‡	3.1972 ex-Thomas Hill	-
16	6w DH	RR; 10275	3' 6"	445hp	1969	12.1982 ex-Thomas Hill	4.1983 to Blue Circle, Holborough
17*	4w DH	S; 10040	3' 2"	229hp	1960	4.1983 ex-RPC Halling	-
18*	4w DH	S; 10035	3' 2"	229hp	1960	4.1983 ex-RPC Halling	-
19	4w DH	RR; 10260	3' 2"	255hp	1966	6.1983 ex-Thomas Hill	out of use by 5.1997; to Staffordshire Locomotives 9.1998
20	4w DH	TH; 164v	2' 8"	179hp	1966	2.1990 ex-RPC Chinnor	5.1998 to Wilmott Bros, Ilkeston
21 (later 2)	0-4-0DE	RH; 434774	3' 2½"	165hp	1961	8.1990 ex-Yorkshire Water	(out of use by 5.1997)
ELIZABETH	0-4-0DE	RH; 412436	3' 2½"	165hp	1958	5.1998 ex-Thompsons	-
No.9	0-4-0DE	RH; 420142	3' 2½"	165hp	1958	7.2000 per Staffordshire Locos	-
	6w DE	GECT 5578			1980	11.2001 ex-Lindsey Refinery	

* Nos.17 and 18 were numbered R13 and R14 respectively until October 1985; they are semi-permanently coupled to run in tandem
¶ Returned to Kempston Hardwick 1945; back to Barrington 5.1947
‡ Thomas Hill rebuild of W/No.127v of 1963
(P) Preserved: RSH 7924 is at the Spa Valley Rly, Tunbridge Wells, where it is now named SOUTHERHAM; AE1875 now at the Colne Valley Railway where it is named BARRINGTON

(b) 2ft gauge

Name/No.	Type	Maker; W/No.	Wheels	Cyls/h.p.	Built	Acquired	Disposal
-	4w DM	OK; ?	?	?	?	?	c.1956; scrapped
-	4w DM	OK; 3444	1' 6"	11hp	1930	?	# 9.1979 (P)
-	4w DM	FH; 1934	1' 5¾"	20hp	1935	New	c.1956 to Eastwoods, Lwr.Halstead
-	0-4-2ST	KS; 1291	2' 0"	7" x 12" (o)	1915	1940 via Hunslet Engine Co	1958; scrapped
No.1	4w DM	MR; 10237	1' 6"	32/42hp	1951	New	c.1969 to Eastwoods, S.Ferriby
-	4w DM	MR; 5945	1' 6"	32/42hp	1937	1952 ex-Marston Valley Brick Co	5.1961 to Eastwoods, Egham
-	4w DM	MR; 5946	1' 6"	32/42hp	1937	1952 ex-Marston Valley Brick Co	c.1961 to Eastwoods, S.Ferriby
No.2	4w DM	MR; 10400	1' 6"	32/42hp	1954	New	c.1968 to Eastwoods, S.Ferriby
No.3	4w DM	MR; 10471	1' 6"	32/42hp	1955	New	c.1969 to Eastwoods, S.Ferriby
-	4w DM	MR; 11111	1' 6"	50hp	1959	New	c.1976 to M.E.Engineering, NW2 (P)
5	4w DM	MR; 11169	1' 6"	50hp	1961	New	1964 to Eastwoods, S.Ferriby
6	4w DM	MR; 11170	1' 6"	50hp	1961	New	c.1965 to Eastwoods, S.Ferriby

Reported derelict 8.1953; remains acquired for preservation 9.1979
(P) Preserved: OK3444 is awaiting restoration at a private location in S.Yorkshire; MR11111 is at the Teifi Valley Railway, Ceredigion

(W/No.1973 of 1927) which until 1968 had worked for the CEGB at Barton Power Station in Lancashire and Sentinel No.7 (W/No.9376 of 1947) which had originally been owned by Ind Coope of Burton-on-Trent but had later been purchased by the NCB and used at East Ardsley Colliery in West Yorkshire. On the Light Railway section, the two Sentinels gave cab rides between the works and the reception sidings. Other rides were also available on a Wickham trolley.

Today
The Barrington Light Railway and the quarry lines are currently running much below their previous past glories, but the system is unique in that the quarry lines are the only standard gauge cement quarry railway system still operational in the United Kingdom.

At the quarry, the north face of the workings which were opened up in 1963 are no longer in use. Instead, the excavation is now concentrated on the east side of the site. The Ruston & Hornsby diesels – the original ones are now 39 years old – handle the quarry traffic.

The inwards coal traffic ceased in the early summer of 1993; it had latterly been imported via Kings Lynn but the closure of the Kings Lynn docks branch brought an end to that. However, the coal traffic resumed in spring 1996. The coal is now imported at Avonmouth, and the current practice is for trains to run as required via either Hitchin or the GE main line, with Acton or Didcot men working as far as Cambridge where Peterborough men take over for the rest of the journey to Foxton.

To accommodate the new system of bulk bottom-discharge wagons at the cement works, a new plant has been constructed on the section of track north of the neck into the works. With a pair of Sentinel locomotives working in tandem, three trains, each of between 12 and 15 wagons, are usually brought up from the exchange sidings each day, a total of around 700 tons daily.

Contributor's note: During the preparation of this article reference was made to an feature by T.B.Peacock in the February 1962 edition of the *Railway Observer* and to R.D.Darvill's article in the June 1987 issue of the *Industrial Railway Record*. Thanks are also due to Messrs. Roger Hateley, Bob Darvill and Bryan L.Wilson for invaluable advice and assistance.

The rail entrance to Barrington Cement Works, 27 February 1960. The photographer is standing almost on the Haslingfield Road level crossing – the old engine shed can be seen behind the lorry on the left and the offices are on the right. Several open wagons stand on the line behind the hedge on the right – this line led to the cement packing and filling sidings. Twenty or so years later, two of the three chimneys had gone – only the middle one remained – and the 'Eastwoods' title had been painted out. PHOTOGRAPH: JOHN R.BONSER

The most significant engineering feature of the Light Railway between the exchange sidings and the cement works was a 235ft long ferro-concrete viaduct over the River Cam. During the summer of 1984 the tandem Sentinel diesels, Nos.17 and 18, cross the viaduct with a train of MGR coal hoppers from the cement works to the exchange sidings. PHOTOGRAPH: IAN P.PEATY

With the shunter on the footsteps, Thomas Hill diesel No.9 approaches the exchange sidings with a train from the cement works – four red bauxite Presflos and half a dozen 16-ton mineral wagons – on 31 August 1967. The chimneys of the cement works can be seen in the distance. PHOTOGRAPH: JOHN R.BONSER

"Why can't it still be steam?" Two youngsters stand at the Foxton Road level crossing and watch Barrington No.9 collect one of the early type of Presflos at the exchange sidings on 31 August 1967. In the distance, a brake van stands on the siding behind the loaded coal wagons. It will be seen that the layout at the exchange sidings had been slightly altered since the 1937 Ordnance Survey map. PHOTOGRAPH: JOHN R.BONSER

Part of the modernisation of the quarry equipment in the 1960s involved the construction of a new wagon tippler. It was photographed on 1 August 1984. The wagon on the tipper is one of the quarry fleet, painted pale green. The track in the foreground is for the locomotive to run round – it had been relaid with 85lb rails in the early 1980s. PHOTOGRAPH: IAN P.PEATY

As noted in the text, in June 1996 two steam locos from the Rutland Railway Museum were used at the Barrington quarries. This is Avonside 0-4-0ST DORA (W/No.1973 of 1927) with a rake of 16-ton steel-bodied wagons in the middle of the quarry on 26 June. She has temporarily moved off the wagons to enable the last one to be loaded. The excavator is a Ruston Bucyrus diesel dragline which was normally used for removing the overburden. This view emphasises the sheer scale of the quarries. PHOTOGRAPH: CLIFF SHEPHERD

It is summer 1984, and dark green-liveried Thomas Hill diesel No.15 returns to the working face with half a dozen empties. PHOTOGRAPH: IAN P. PEATY

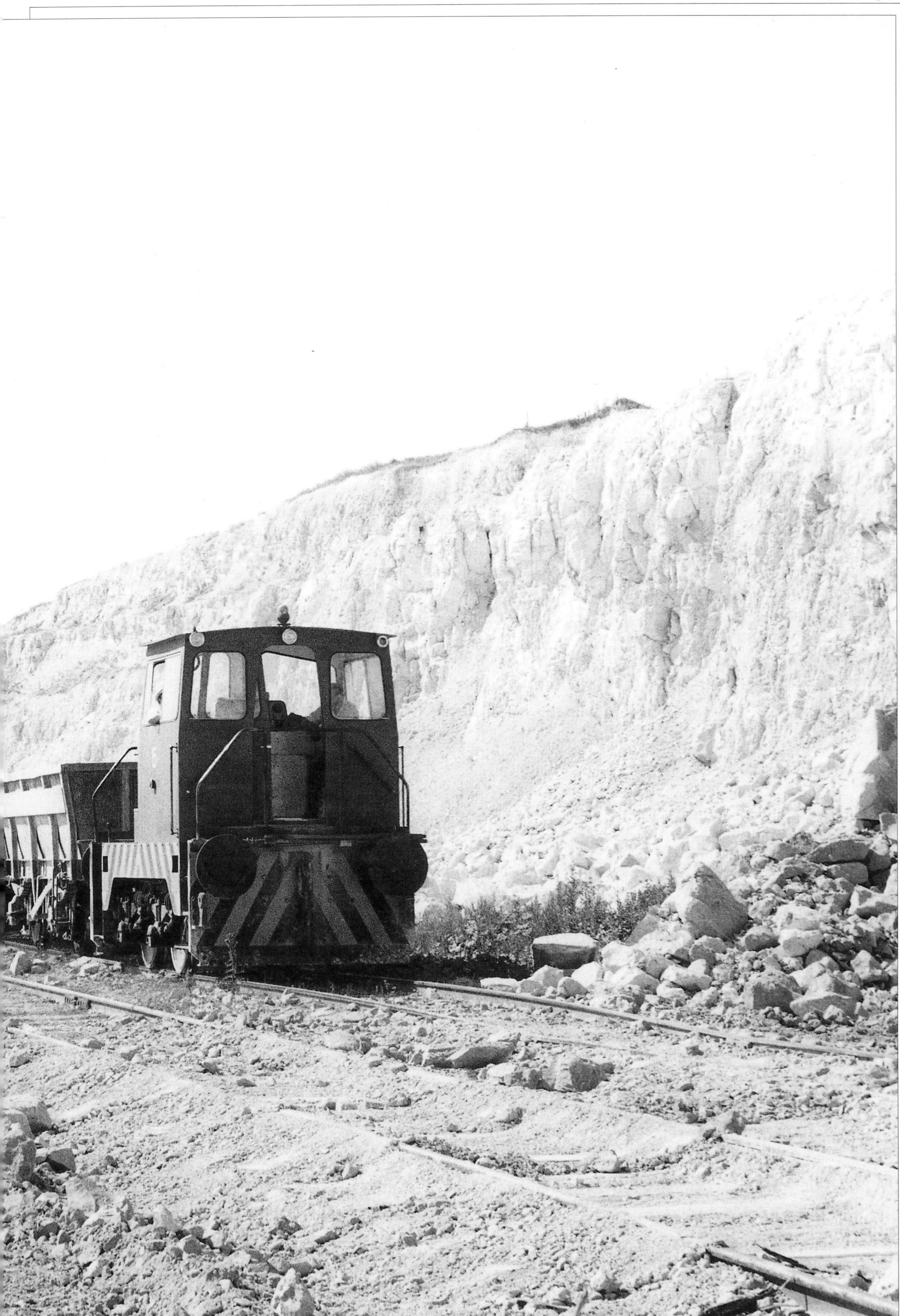

The other Rutland Museum engine which worked at Barrington on 26 June 1996 was Sentinel W/No.9376 of 1947. Here it is in charge of three of the earlier type of 16-ton wagons which are being loaded by the Ruston Bucyrus excavator at the chalk face. It should be emphasised that this and the other picture of the 'steam specials' of June 1996 show the locomotives undertaking ordinary, everyday quarry duties – the workings were *not* posed. PHOTOGRAPH: CLIFF SHEPHERD

Today, under ordinary circumstances the railway work at the quarry is performed by the Ruston & Hornsby diesels. This is No.8 taking empty wagons to the loading point at the quarry on 26 June 1996. Seven or eight wagons are the usual train load from the quarries to the works. PHOTOGRAPH: CLIFF SHEPHERD

Ruston & Hornsby No.7 approaches the tippler with a rake of loaded wagons on 26 June 1996. The tall light standard on the right enabled work to continue on dark winter afternoons. The pile of rails and sleepers are ready to be laid where and when required; this was a common procedure at quarries – as the working faces of the quarry shifted, railway track was repositioned accordingly. PHOTOGRAPH: CLIFF SHEPHERD

Ruston & Hornsby No.8 waits with a single wagon on standby for the track-laying gang who are lifting track for a new alignment to the working face. The gantry carries electric cables over the track – as the sidings were regularly repositioned, the gantries enabled the cables to be moved while being kept well above 'train' height. PHOTOGRAPH: IAN P. PEATY

BOTH SIDES OF THE DART
Photographs by John R. Bonser; captions by Mike Thresher

Left. In railway terms, Kingswear in south Devon was a bit of a contradiction. It was the terminus of a steeply-graded single-track line and served a community with a population of only about 800, but it hosted through expresses to Paddington (including two named trains), some of which were hauled by the GWR's finest – the Kings. One of the main reasons for this unusual state of affairs was that Kingswear was the station for Dartmouth. Largely because of opposition from a local landowner, the GWR had been unable to build the railway into Dartmouth itself so it built the line, instead, to Kingswear, on the opposite side of the River Dart and provided a ferry service between Kingswear and Dartmouth. From 1908 the ferry service was provided by THE MEW, the famous little vessel which was the subject of an article in *Railway Bylines 7:3,* but although THE MEW was an attraction in its own right it was not the only attraction at Dartmouth, as this splendid view confirms. The station – a modeller's delight, with the possible exception of the very lengthy platform – is wedged in between Fore Street and the river bank. The sidings on the quay seem not to be over-used, but at one time they had dealt with a considerable amount of bulk coal traffic. A fair proportion of the coal came in by sea from Goole to be taken on by rail to Torquay Gas Works, while smaller quantities were transferred by barge to be taken across the river to Dartmouth Gas Works. Just beyond the far end of the wharf can be seen the landing stage (with the shelter with the curved roof) which was used by THE MEW. On the opposite bank of the river, the attractive little town of Dartmouth is spread out on the lower slopes of the hill. This picture was taken on Thursday 20 June 1957. It is clearly a 'Bylines' part of the evening at Kingswear – no Kings or named trains, but smaller engines and secondary trains. We have a 51XX 2-6-2T waiting with the 8.00pm to Newton Abbot (where it will connect with a Penzance-Manchester train) and 43XX 7316 with the 8.45pm to Exeter. Magnificent!

Below left. 5105 leaves Kingswear with the 7.20pm to Exeter on 20 June 1957. The station is out of view to the right – the coaches in the distance on the right are stabled in the carriage sidings about ¼-mile north of the station.

Below. About ¾-mile north of Kingswear station, Britannia Halt was opened in 1898 to serve the Naval College on the opposite bank of the river. In 1917 the halt was renamed Kingswear Crossing, but was later renamed again, this time as Steam Ferry Crossing. Although the halt remained in use until BR days it never appeared in the public timetables (until being taken over by the Torbay Steam Railway, that is). This picture of the halt and the delightfully-titled Steam Ferry Crossing Ground Frame was taken on 20 June 1957. The road crossing the line immediately beyond the halt is the A379. The halt was served by some of the local trains, there being a ferry service from just behind the halt to the college. When it came to the beginning and end of term at the Naval College, special trains – often 8 or 9 corridor coaches plus up to three vans for the mountain of luggage – ran between Kingswear (*not* the halt!) and Paddington. For outgoing trains, the luggage was sent a few days in advance, being taken across by THE MEW from Dartmouth to Kingswear. As for the railway line itself, north of Steam Ferry Halt it embarked on a climb of 1 in 66 to Churston, then dropped on a ruling gradient of 1 in 60 to Paignton.

The Steam Ferry – also known as Dartmouth Higher Ferry – sets out on the short crossing from Britannia Halt to Dartmouth on 20 June 1957. The vessel, a paddle steamer which ran on guide wires, had been built in 1921 and was owned and operated by Messrs. Philip & Sons.

Photographer John Bonser returned to Kingswear on 2 June 1970. By this time the once-proud station had seen the effects of 'rationalisation' – all the quayside sidings had been lifted and, although the lines on the east side of the platform were still in situ, they had been officially taken out of use some eighteen months previously. The loco and carriage sidings to the north of the station had also been taken out of use, so Kingswear's entire railway layout now comprised only the one platform road and the run-round loop. Nevertheless, the station was still open – and that was more than could be said of many other stations by this time. In 1972 BR sold the Paignton-Kingswear section of line to the Dartmouth & Torbay Railway, so Kingswear once again became a destination for steam-hauled trains.

We're looking out from the dead-end at Kingswear on the evening of 2 June 1970. In the distance can be seen the footbridge which connected Fore Street to the quay – this bridge was a hugely popular vantage point for generations of railway photographers (including John Bonser!).

Finally, we venture across the river to Dartmouth which was well known as the town with a railway station but no trains. The 'station' was served by the ferries to/from Kingswear but was, in fact, little more than a booking office and waiting hall. This picture was taken on 2 June 1970; despite appearances the premises *were* still operational at this time. An Austin 1800 – hmmm... Tremendous leg room front and rear, comfortable, economical, but a typical BMC 'pudding-stirrer' gear stick – at least, that's how the editor remembers his!

FOURUM – The Far Tottering and Oyster Creek Railway
Photographs by H.C.Casserley

For the Festival of Britain in the summer of 1951, the 'Far Tottering & Oyster Creek Railway' was laid out in Battersea Park. Our pictures of the railway were all taken on 16 August of that year. Whereas the Festival of Britain itself drew to a close in September 1951, the 'FT&OC' remained in operation at Battersea for a couple of years longer. Our knowledge of the 'FT&OC' is embarrassingly thin, but we seem to recall that the intention was for the railway to become a permanent fixture at Battersea, only for a serious accident to result in its closure at the end of the 1953 season. (If we're hopelessly adrift with that comment, we hope someone will put us right!)

For working the 'FT&OC', three diesel-engined locomotives were supplied by H.D.Barlow of Southport. But they did not look like any ordinary diesel locomotives – their bodies were designed by the legendary Roland Emmett. The upper picture on the facing page shows No.1 *Nellie*, a real 'Emmett-meets-Heath-Robinson' vision. The lower picture opposite shows No.2 *Neptune* which seems to be a cross between a paddle steamer and something from the very earliest days of railways. The upper picture on this page is of No.3 *Wild Goose* which appears to be modelled on an airship. Below is a view of 'Oyster Creek' station. To the best of our meagre knowledge, the three locomotives were returned to Barlow's of Southport at the end of the 1953 season and were fitted with more conventional 'steam outline' bodies before being resold for use elsewhere.

CROSS HANDS AND TUMBLE
Photographs by Andrew Muckley; commentary by Bryan L. Wilson

The last of the 16XX pannier tanks – in numerical terms, that is – was No.1669. Here it waits to leave Burry Port (BPGV) station yard with its wagon-loads of mischief on 25 September 1965. The train consisted of 10 vacuum-fitted hyfits and two brake vans. The human cargo was all in the first three wagons so they could savour the smell and the soot. And, yes – it rained as well. No.1669 had, in its short 10½-year life, worked at Bristol, Wrexham GC, Southall, Whitland, Carmarthen and Neath as well as Llanelly. It was condemned 6 days after this trip. Note the class 'B' passenger headcode. Burry Port BPGV station had closed on 21 September 1953 when the old BPGV line to Cwmmawr had lost its passenger services.

Cross Hands and Tumble… No, this is not an old South Wales Morris Dance. It is, in fact, just two of the destinations which were visited by a joint Railway Correspondence & Travel Society and Stephenson Locomotive Society rail tour on Saturday 25 September 1965.

Cross Hands was the terminus of the old Llanelly & Mynydd Mawr mineral line from Llanelly, and Tumble was the last station before the terminus. The line never had a public passenger service, but that is not to say that passengers were never conveyed. Indeed, on 6 June 1881, 1,000 souls were conveyed to Cross Hands in two trains – one formed of sixteen wagons and the other of about eight – for a grand picnic party, the 'tea ticket' including the train journey. There was a somewhat less jolly outing in 1893 when police were conveyed by train to Tumble during a

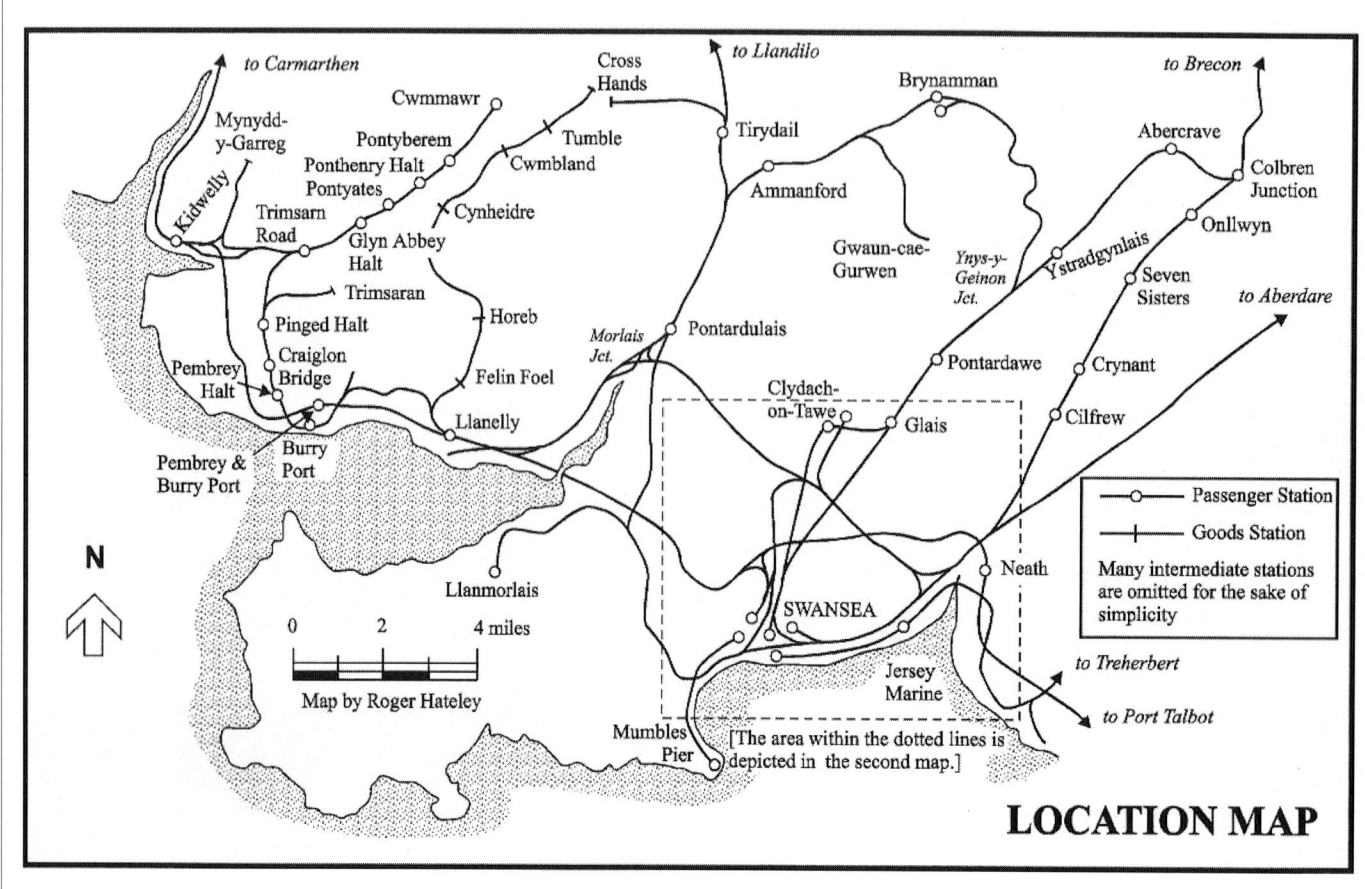

LOCATION MAP

SWANSEA DISTRICT

Map by Roger Hateley

Many intermediate stations are omitted for the sake of simplicity

a - South Dock
b - East or Prince of Wales Dock
c - Kings Dock
d - Queens Docks

---

miners' strike. The proprietors of Great Mountain Colliery at Tumble had brought in hundreds of miners from Scotland and the North of England and had provided homes for more than 100 of them – this greatly displeased the locals, hence the industrial action. The picknickers of 1881 and the police in 1893 were conveyed in open wagons and, as if to revive the custom of conveying freight-rated passengers, the RCTS/SLS railtour of 1965 included 'open wagon' transportation, not only to Tumble, but also to Cwmmawr on the nearby Burry Port & Gwendraeth Valleys line.

Pontyates, on the old BPGV line – less than eight miles out and we need a drink. One of the first finds of the rail tour was this GWR Wolverhampton-built water crane dated August 1887. And another thing... Who said lady guards were a recent innovation?

The end of the BPGV line at Cwmmawr. The driver doesn't look too cheerful but 'Black Mac', in his smart shoes, is happy to pose for the camera. Beyond the engine, just look at the lengths some people went to just to complete their coverage of the line. The road in the background was the start of the walk uphill to Tumble.

We are now up on the Llanelly & Mynydd Mawr line at the Cross Hands terminus. The line here was, according to the directors, '...considered to be open for public traffic from 1 January 1883'. The L&MMR was, in effect, a contractor's railway but, as such, it lasted rather well. It was taken into the GWR fold on 1 January 1923 and, although the two-mile section at the top of the line between Cross Hands and Tumble was abandoned in October 1966, the rest of the line remained in use for the traffic from Cynheidre Colliery until March 1989. No.1643 is the pannier in charge. In contrast to the peripatetic 1669, this was always a Neath Division engine. However, 1643 also had only six days service left. The Inspector has done his job and the hand points are secured by clamp, seen in the left-hand corner.

The rail tour emanated from Swansea, its timing being intended to celebrate – if that is the right word – the end of steam in south-west Wales. Indeed, Llanelly shed closed on 4 October 1965, just nine days after the tour. One of the attractions of the tour was that it covered some rather interesting 'goods only' lines. Very few, if any, of the rail tour participants would have previously travelled on these lines and, as 1965 was the time when the Beeching Report was being implemented, a number of these lines would not be around for much longer. The tour therefore offered a number of 'last chances'.

The RCTS/SLS party gathered in Swansea on the evening of Friday 24 September. A recent mention of the tour (in the October 2000 issue of the *Railway Observer*) commented that most of the participants '...stayed at the Mackworth Hotel, a very basic commercial hotel since demolished, for in those days hotel accommodation in West Wales was very limited'.

A ticket for the rail tour cost 60 shillings (£3.00). The tour started from Swansea High Street on Saturday morning, 0-6-0PTs Nos.3654 and 9609 hauling the train to Sandy Junction at Llanelly. Here the participants had the opportunity to view locomotives at the Llanelly Steel Company's works and to visit the open hearth operations. Eleven steam locomotives were on site including open-cab Barclay 0-4-0STs NORA, LINDSAY, VICTORY and CHRISTOPHER.

Having visited the steel works the party divided. Half joined the train of open wagons and, with Pannier No.1643 in charge, journeyed up the entire length (almost 13 miles) of the L&MM line to Cross Hands, then back down as far as Tumble. Here they dismounted and then walked the mile to Cwmmawr, the terminus of the Burry Port & Gwendraeth Valley branch. This line had once had scheduled passenger services, but they had been withdrawn in September 1953. At Cwmmawr the party found another 16XX, No.1669, waiting with a train of open wagons. This was their means of conveyance back down the 13-mile-long branch to Burry Port station.

Meanwhile, the other half of the party rejoined the 'main train' at Llanelly and, with No.9609 in charge, continued to Burry Port. Here they took the 'wagon train' up to Cwmmawr. They continued from there the 'other way round' – i.e. walk to Tumble, then take the other 'wagon train' back to Llanelly.

Thus, No.9609 and the 'main train' were waiting at Pembrey & Burry Port to pick up the first half of the party and to take them back to Llanelly for the obligatory visit to the engine shed. The second half, having arrived from Tumble, rejoined the 'main train'. For the return leg from Llanelly No.9609 was reunited with No.3654 for the journey from Morfa Junction to Morlais Junction and the Swansea District Line, continuing via Felin Fran and the curve to Jersey Marine Junction South. Here the engines ran round in preparation for the next stage of the tour.

This next stage was up the Vale of Neath line to Riverside station, then via the Neath & Brecon line to Colbren Junction. Its must have been a very long time since a train with buffet facilities had been seen at this outpost! The train then returned to Swansea via the Midland route, passing Ynysygeinon Junction, by-passing Swansea St.Thomas, and continuing via East Dock, Jersey Marine (again), Felin Fran West and the Morriston Low Level line to Swansea High Street.

That was the end of Day One. The following day Fishguard and Milford Haven were visited, giving another 'last chance' to go to these places by 'proper' steam power. Our photographs all come from Day One, but for that we offer neither excuse nor apology. Day One was without doubt the more interesting of the two days on account of the obscure 'goods only' lines which were traversed.

No.1643 approaches Tumble from Cross Hands. This is a very rare view of rail-borne passengers up here, and the train seems to have brought a few trespassers to the lineside as well. The GWR practice of hanging a bucket on the back of the bunker is one for modellers intent on ultra-realism.

A close-up of the human cargo approaching Tumble. Does anyone recognise themselves? Or any of the other participants? Someone you have recently been next to in the pension queue at the Post Office perhaps? After all, this was 36 years ago!

The origins of the L&MM line lay in the 4ft gauge Carmarthenshire Railway which received its Act of Parliament in 1802. This was only the second Act of Parliament promoting a public railway in Britain. (We knew you were going to ask – the first was the Surrey Iron Railway.) However, despite its historic status the Carmarthenshire Railway closed in 1844. It was left to moulder until April 1880 when the L&MM converted it to the standard gauge and generally upgraded it in the process. It reopened in January 1883. When the 'super pit' at Cynheidre was developed in the 1950s the line was partly realigned to cater for increased loads and the use of the hefty 42XX 2-8-0Ts. One of the improvements was this cutting, blasted out of sheer rock at Quarry Mawr, south of Cynheidre. Quarry Mawr, incidentally, had provided stone for the reconstruction of the line in the 1880s.

The L&MM line abounded in steep gradients (the steepest was 1 in 44) and sharp curves. Here, 1643 negotiates one of the curves on the approach to Llanelly. This is classic 1960s rail tour stuff – tidy trousers, mackintoshes, and people taking pictures of each other with the engine in the background. But just what is that fellow in the first wagon looking at?

Three working 'matchboxes' are together at Llanelly shed, very probably for the last time. The two in the foreground are Nos.3654 (the other rail tour engine) and 4676. In the background, 9609 is on the rail tour train; the train is standing on the connection from the original Llanelly Dock station which closed as long ago as 1 September 1879. The first coach behind 9609 is of SR origin. Could this have been the first visit of an SR coach to Llanelly shed?

One last look from Llanelly shed sidings as 9609 comes off shed to rejoin 3654 at the front of the tour train. Morfa Junction signal box is prominent. The remains of Morfa Tinplate Works are to the left of the 'box.

The shed visit completed, we're ready to head off again. We are looking east towards Llandeilo Juntion. Morfa Junction signal box is ahead.

The journey back to Swansea went past Felin Fran halt. The halt had been in business from 2 January 1922 until 11 June 1956 and had been the terminating point for many of the services from Swansea High Street via the Morriston Low Level line. Here we are looking south-west. The junction for the Clydach North branch is behind the photographer. Ahead of us, the signal on the down side still has the bracket but no arm, the direct facing connection which it protected having been taken out the previous year. In the distance we see the water tank at Felin Fran sidings. This was the point where the Whitland-Kensington milk trains changed engines.

By the 1960s, Jersey Marine Junction South was the sort of place that one could get to only by rail tour. It had once been traversed by passenger trains to and from East Dock station, but they had ceased in the 1930s and, since then, the line had been used for goods only. The junction was the point where the Vale of Neath and the Rhondda & Swansea Bay lines connected; there were also connections to Jersey Marine South sidings. Here we are looking east – Swansea is to the right and Neath to the left. The two rail tour engines are running round the train in readiness for the next stage, bunkers-first up the Neath & Brecon line. The handsome McKenzie & Holland signal box, incidentally, was opened on 26 October 1926. It came to Jersey Marine 'secondhand', having previously been sited – or so it is believed – at Danygraig Junction. At Jersey Marine, its frame was extended from 38 to 54 levers in 1933 when the new double-line junction was laid between the old VoN and R&SB lines.

Neath Riverside station on the N&B line had closed in June 1964 – a year and a week before the rail tour. Even when the line had been in its heyday (though, in the case of the N&B passenger services, 'heyday' is a relative term), the sight of standard coaching stock including a miniature buffet would have raised a few eyebrows. The tour train has been hauled from Jersey Marine by the two Panniers and will continue – with the engines bunker-first – up the Neath & Brecon line. Here we are looking south towards Jersey Marine. Out of view behind the photographer, the ex-GWR main line crosses the N&B line just beyond the north end of the Riverside platforms. A Western Welsh single-decker is crossing the road bridge in the mid-distance.

Looking in the other direction at Riverside. The overbridge carries the South Wales main line (Swansea to the left and Neath General to the right).

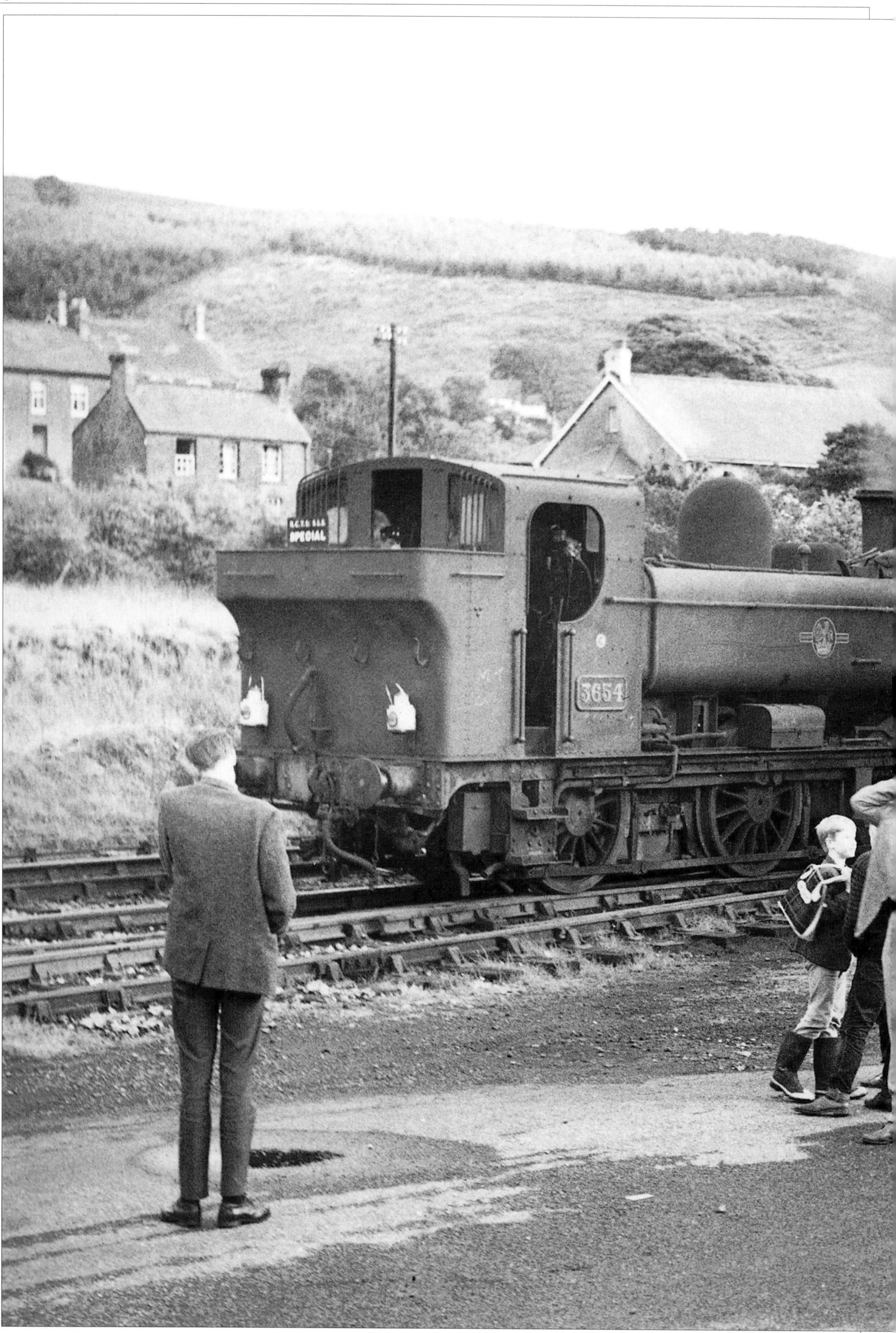
SPECIAL
3654

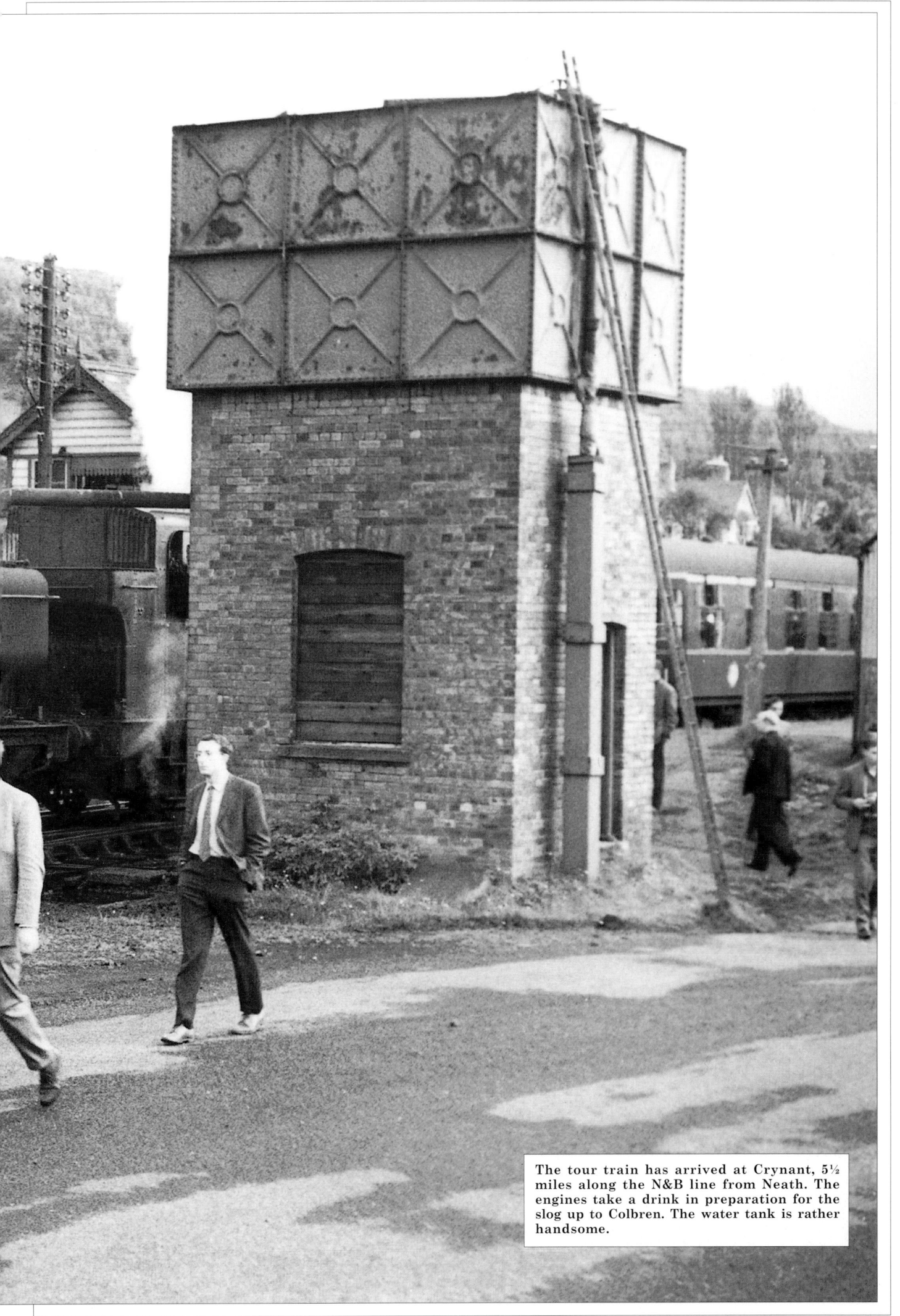

The tour train has arrived at Crynant, 5½ miles along the N&B line from Neath. The engines take a drink in preparation for the slog up to Colbren. The water tank is rather handsome.

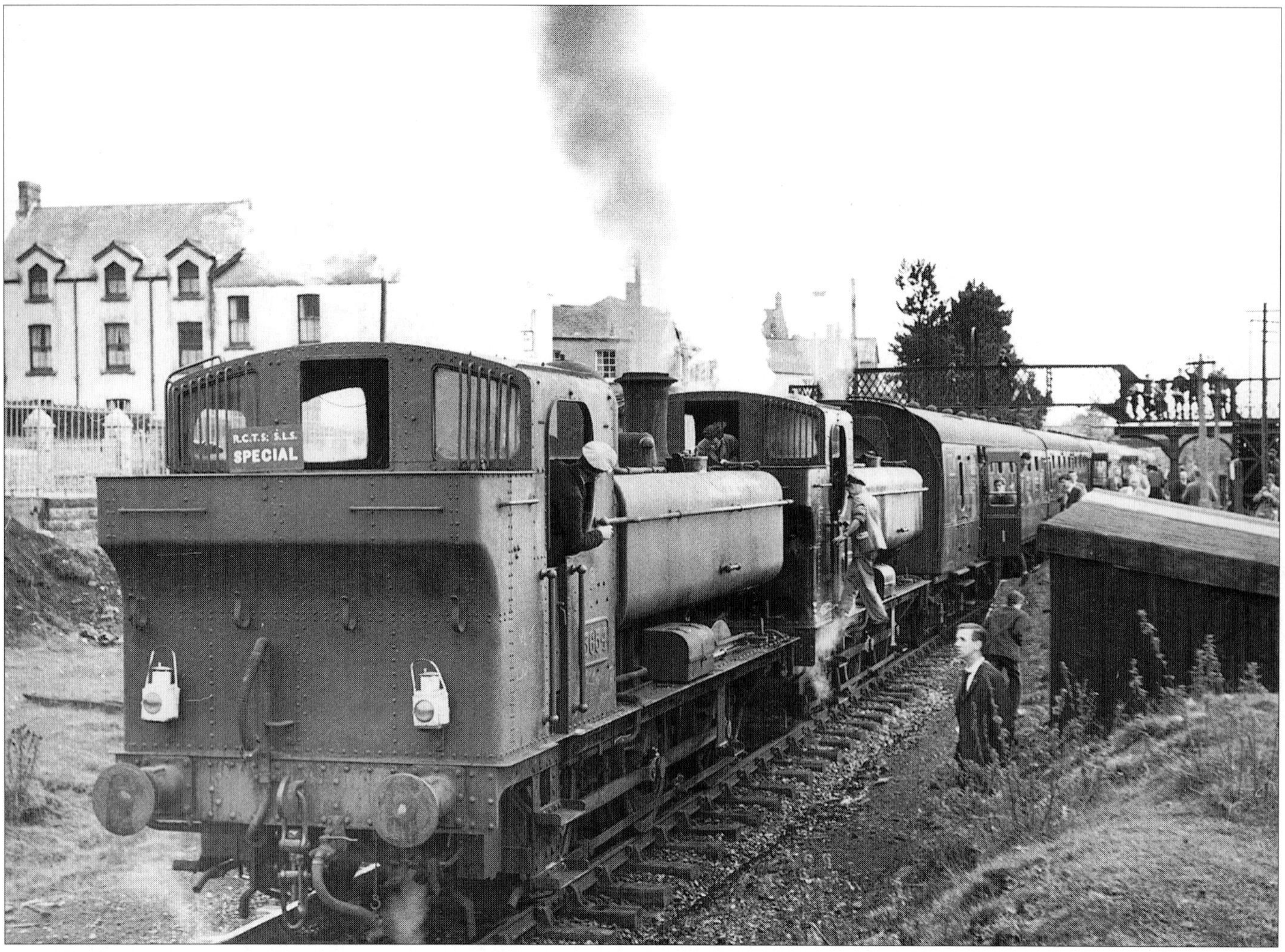
R.C.T.S. S.L.S.
SPECIAL

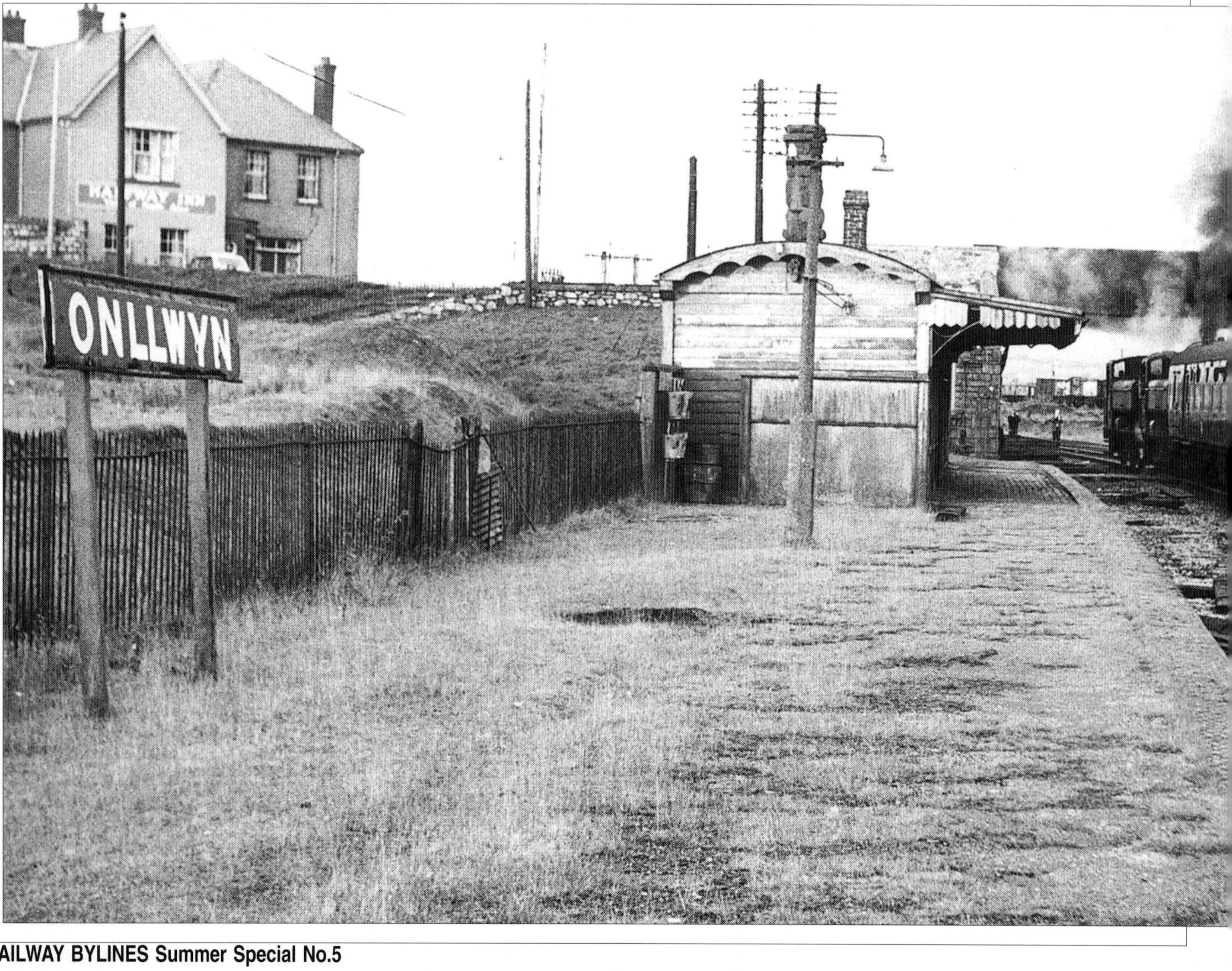
ONLLWYN

Above. Colbren Junction, looking north towards Sennybridge & Devynock. The tour train has deposited its entourage at the N&B line platform (behind the platform on the right) and is heading up the line for a short distance before reversing back into the Ynys-y-Geinon line platform (the one on the right). This platform had last been used for public passenger services in 1932 – the LMS had run trains through to Swansea until the end of 1930, but the GWR had maintained a service as far as Ystradygynlais until 12 September 1932. Clearly, Colbren Junction had never been envisaged as a major passenger interchange; the station and its buildings are somewhat rudimentary, being the archetypal N&B 'gypsy caravan' on the right and little more than a glorified hen house on the left. A couple of points of special interest: firstly the McKenzie & Holland signal box of 1873 and, secondly, the ferocious gradient of the Brecon line (left of centre in the distance, beyond the signals). And so we returned to Swansea, some to go home, others to await the trip to Fishguard the following day. A few more lines would be marked off as 'done' and a few more engines seen, but the greatest satisfaction for most would be seeing, first-hand, some truly fascinating corners of the local railway network. And behind steam, to boot. This trip would never be possible again.

Top left. On its way up to Colbren the tour train stops at Seven Sisters. This was rather a far cry from its namesake in North-east London. The stop here had been arranged principally for photography but, clearly, many passengers preferred simply to observe and to soak up the atmosphere of an unsung rural railway.

Bottom left. Onllwyn had a typical Neath & Brecon station building which was once described by Harold Morgan of the Welsh Railways Research Circle as '...built of timber with a clap-boarded exterior and a distinctive roof profile – somewhat reminiscent of a gypsy caravan'. The enamel sign – blue with white letters – is also typical N&B.

TWO PORTRAITS AND A PAIR OF INTERESTING ANGLES

In 1932/33 four ex-LB&SCR E1 0-6-0Ts were transferred to the Isle of Wight principally to work the heavier goods trains. One of the quartet was SR No.B152 which was transferred to the island in July 1932 to become No.2 YARMOUTH. Prior to transfer the engine was fitted with a new boiler and repainted green, as evidenced in this portrait which was taken at Newport shed in 1933.

The longest-lived of the four Isle of Wight E1s was No.4 WROXALL which was not withdrawn until October 1960. All four of the engines spent most of their BR lives allocated to Newport shed, but that shed closed in 1957 and the two surviving E1s (Nos.3 and 4) were duly transferred to Ryde. By this time they had become rather shabby – this was in marked contrast to the island's O2s. This picture of the none-too-glamorous No.4 was taken at Ryde shed yard on 25 May 1958. PHOTOGRAPH: PETER GROOM

Not exactly what one thinks of as a standard 'loco picture', but an intriguing angle nonetheless... This is No.3 RYDE in Newport shed yard on 7 July 1955. PHOTOGRAPH: PHILIP KELLEY

Now, if you thought the picture above was a bit of an unusual angle, how about this? This delightful 'over the fence' picture shows No.1 MEDINA at the back of the coal stage road at Ryde shed. Fascinating! PHOTOGRAPH: DEREK CLAYTON

THE CUCKOO, THE COFFIN AND THE CHRISTMAS TREES
Adapted by Anthony P. Vent

Hubert Hobden began his railway career in 1913, joining the LB&SCR as a shed cleaner at Eastbourne depot. In these extracts from his unpublished memoirs he relates his recollections of the now closed 'Cuckoo Line' – the single line between Polegate and Red Mill Junction in East Sussex which took its name from the annual fair at Heathfield – which was one of his regular duties as a fireman and driver during the 1920s. In 1935, following the electrification of the line to Eastbourne and Hastings, Mr.Hobden transferred to the new E.M.U. depot at Ore as a motorman. He retired in 1961.

While working as a driver from 1924-28, I was not on any link working – instead, I covered for special trains and sickness. My turns of duty were frequently altered, the new instructions being by hand-delivered notes. On one occasion we had a 'call on' for 12.30pm to prepare an engine to run light to Polegate at 1.30. On arriving at Polegate we were turned into the East Sidings on to an 18-wagon train loaded with broken concrete for Rotherfield. This load was the maximum for the gradients. The guard, a Lewes man, was not over familiar with the 'Cuckoo Line'. We had no worry about the water supply as we had a large-boilered 'Vulcan' (a C2X 0-6-0) with a full tender. I had an able fireman who had recently transferred from Battersea having been made redundant by the spread of electrification. He was not fully conversant with the heavy gradients but was skilled in firing. Before leaving the depot I had examined the notices and also the permanent way instructions issued about relaying.

In these was a note about relay work between Heathfield and Mayfield, between trains. We were working a special train and no notification on timing was issued, other than to signalmen on the route – the timing we had to adhere to was from the normal sectional freight train schedule. Drawing away from the East Sidings, and away through the down loop line, we found that the train was heavy.

On the first gradient to Waldron & Horeham Road, as the station was then called (it wasn't renamed Waldron & Horam until 1935), we lost four minutes. Having to slow down at this station to change the staff gave us no chance to get a running start at the 1 in 50 facing us. Nevertheless, the engine kept plodding slowly all the way to Heathfield but, by the time that we arrived there, another 23 minutes were lost. At the steepest point on this section was a religious poster on a wall: "Come unto me all you who are heavy laden and I will give ye rest", it proclaimed. This had been up for months and some of us reckoned it wasn't entirely a coincidence! Anyway, we carried on and, after leaving Heathfield, we were on a curving downhill gradient of 1 in 52. After pulling away through the tunnel the heavy wagons started to push us faster. "Pull your hand brake on hard", I said. "I've got it on as hard as I can get it", replied my mate. I then gave him assistance with the Westinghouse brake, but it made no difference. Our speed was rapidly increasing. We had now reached about 30mph and, not far off, was the 15mph speed limit for the relaying work. I was absolutely powerless to reduce our gallop – and the train was still gaining. My only hope now was the guard. I grabbed hold of the whistle valve and gave him a series of the 'cock-a-doodle-doo' whistles. These would also warn the platelayers, for my mind was well ahead – indeed, I was wondering if they had left a rail unscotched or a tieplate unbolted. My mate, alarmed, came over and said "What are you doing that for?" I told him that it was partly to warn the platelayers, and he immediately crossed over to his side of the footplate and got out onto the running board. "What the heck are you out there for, George?" I asked. He replied that he was getting ready to jump.

At the same moment the gang came into sight, standing on top of the cutting bank. I saw the ganger standing out well in sight, signalling to me that it was safe. We passed the gang with a *whoosh* and

Left. Mayfield station was an attractive establishment – small but substantially constructed – serving a community of some 3,000 souls. Coming from the south, there was a gradient on the approach to the station. It was on this gradient that Hubert Hobden's goods train nearly came to grief in the 1920s... PHOTOGRAPH: ANTHONY VENT COLLECTION

Below. 'Vulcan' C2 No.543 was rebuilt as a C2X in 1915 and was one of four of the class allocated to Eastbourne in 1925. When working with this very engine on the 2.45pm Tunbridge Wells West-Polegate goods, Hubert Hobden had a bit of a mishap. While shunting at Horeham Road three wagons were derailed – this was due to three sacks of corn which had fallen from a goods wagon and come to rest across the rails. This episode closed the Cuckoo Line for several hours, much to the frustration of the local railway staff. The Eastbourne locomotive foreman was none to pleased either, as he had to be called out with the breakdown tool van. As for the engine, it survived until 1960 as BR No.32543. PHOTOGRAPH: ANTHONY VENT COLLECTION

the train continued, out of control, down to the bottom of the gradient. The train sped out onto the level and on the sharp curve which preceded the up gradient to Mayfield. My mate, who had now recovered a little from his panic, was struggling to release the hand brake. I went across to help him but the friction had caused the iron brake blocks to expand to such a degree that it was impossible to release them. We were now on an up gradient of 1 in 48 and, with the tender brake hard on, we soon came to a stand. "Let them cool off, George", I said. "I'll go back and see the guard".

On reaching the guard's van I called out to him "Hadn't you got the hand brake on?" He replied that he had been trying to make up some of the time lost at Heathfield. I explained to him that the train had been out of control and that he now had to wait until our brake blocks cooled down. He grinned like a Cheshire Cat. I was convinced that he had been having a snooze.

We eventually managed to release the brake and continued on to Rotherfield, After shunting the train into the back road there, we returned to Polegate with the brake van and guard. The brake van was shunted into the West Sidings. The guard handed me my journal and said "So long!" No other words were uttered. A few days later I saw the ganger, Arthur Franks, and mentioned the incident. "I heard you coming, Bert, and told my men to get out of the bloody way", he said dryly.

Off the rails

Serious accidents were, mercifully, very few and far between. However, when I was on a passenger duty with 0-4-2T No.616 on 19 April 1920, there was a fairly minor mishap at Heathfield. My driver and I were booked to work the 6.20pm Eastbourne-Heathfield, a pleasant evening run. On arrival at Heathfield we ran round our train then shunted it into the dock road and picked up two vans loaded with chickens. On this duty, the familiar chicken 'peds' (the Sussex name for special boxes made locally to hold 1-2 dozen carcasses for the London markets) with the markings of local chicken fatteners were always to be seen. The local carrier collected and brought these 'peds' to the station and loaded them onto the 'chicken express' which was due to leave Heathfield at 9.20pm. It was essential that it left on time so that the chicken vans could be attached to the London train at Polegate. We had finished our shunting and had taken water and were awaiting the arrival of the 7.30pm from Tunbridge Wells.

The Eastbourne tool van, which came to the rescue of Hubert Hodben's train at Horeham Road. This was not Mr. Hobden's first encounter with the tool van – not by a very long chalk. In 1913 – just twelve days after the had started work as a cleaner at Eastbourne shed – he had been called out to join the tool van in the rescue of a down train which had derailed south of Hailsham. The derailment had been caused by children placing stones between the running rail and the check rail at an occupation crossing. This picture of the oft used van is believed to have been taken in the early 1920s though, as always, we stand to be corrected. PHOTOGRAPH: ANTHONY VENT COLLECTION

'Old Ned', the Heathfield signalman, had rung his hand bell from the signal box and was on the platform ready to change the staff. After a few words with 'Old Levi', the driver of the down train, and a cheery "Your turn next" to us, he walked to his box. He was in his cabin before the down train had started. We heard Levi give a pop on his whistle and, as he passed, he gave my mate and myself his customary "Hello! So long!" and was off. When his engine was opposite the signal box, he was really 'off' – off the rails, that is.

His train had derailed right across our exit and we were trapped in the dock road. There was nothing we could do but wait. The fire was drawn back under the door to stop the steam pressure from rising too high. Arrangements were soon made for the breakdown vans and crew to be summoned, but it was an inconvenient time for the fitters and any casual staff would have been off duty. Consequently, it was around 10.30pm before we had any sign that the breakdown vans were approaching.

My mate and I were sitting in the cab when a voice from the platform asked if anyone was injured. In the dim light of the fire I recognised the local doctor. We invited him to step into the cab. He lit his pipe and said "Don't you men have a smoke?" We explained that we had not been smoking for fear of being censured by any superiors who might be on the breakdown vans. "Rubbish!", said the doctor. "Nothing better for a man's nerves than a good smoke!"

Fortunately, the engine was soon rerailed and moved, leaving us to follow as soon as the section was clear.

Mention was made earlier of the Heathfield signalman, 'Old Ned', ringing his hand bell. This was an old LB&SCR custom to herald the approach of a passenger train. Heathfield was the last station on the LB&SCR to retain this tradition. The polished brass bell was about 7" in diameter at the mouth, with an 8" walnut handle. It stood reverently at the signal cabin door on a piece of coconut matting. I wonder what became of it?

Trees and rabbits

Going back to 1920 – when I was a fireman – I was booked on local freight and shunting duties with a regular driver, known to one and all as 'Squeaker' and, on one particular December day, we were working the 2.45pm freight from Tunbridge Wells to Polegate. 'Squeaker' had a family of four and, as it was nearing Christmas, he wanted to get them a tree. This gave the rest of us the same idea and, after we had talked with the guard, we decided that we should *all* have a tree. We had seen some small seedlings, about three feet high, growing in the cutting between Heathfield and Mayfield and so 'Squeaker' made arrangements with the guard to push on with the Mayfield shunting and get away in good time so that, when we reached the trees, we had time to stop the train. I was left in charge while 'Squeaker' and the guard climbed up the bank and pulled up some of the trees. They soon returned, throwing them up into the bunker. We proceeded to Heathfield, keeping things to ourselves.

Those days were full of similar incidents. My mate would, if he spotted a farmer near the track, throw up a note tied to a piece of coal, ordering a brace of rabbits. The note would give the time of our return and, almost without fail, on our return a brace would be held up in a forked stick so that we could snatch them as we passed. Attached to the rabbits was a note giving the price and our instructions – "pay the signalman", or similar. At that time the going price for a rabbit was 6d.

The coffin

And then there was the story of the coffin. I was not involved in this incident – I heard the tale during my early 'Cuckoo Line' days… 'Bunny' was a passenger guard and he was always up to some prank or other. On the day in question he was working the 6.45pm Tunbridge Wells West-Eastbourne which was carrying a coffin in the van at the front of the train. A coffin was not an unusual 'parcel' on a down train and, to avoid delay at the destination – in this case Heathfield – a message was telephoned from the previous station (Mayfield) to advise that the 'parcel' was on its way. Before reaching Heathfield, 'Bunny' climbed up on to the parcels shelf in his van and lay down behind the coffin. On arrival at the station the porter opened the van door and went in. In the dim gas light he saw the coffin and walked over to it. Bunny immediately began drumming his heels on the shelf and moaned "Let me out, let me out!" The porter – a nervous young chap – bolted. He sprinted along the platform, desperately looking for someone to help him in this time of extreme stress. He found a bystander and garbled, "There's somebody alive in the coffin". Another member of the station staff was summoned. He ventured gingerly towards the van only to find a grinning Bunny standing alongside the coffin. The story made its way up and down the line, no doubt embellished each time it was told!

Right. LB&SCR cleaner, fireman and driver, Hubert Hobden. This studio portrait of young Mr. Hobden was taken during his time as a cleaner at Eastbourne shed and, apparently, the sartorial tips for the studio session came from his landlady's son, a waiter in a posh local hotel. PHOTOGRAPH: ANTHONY VENT COLLECTION

Below. D1 0-4-2T No.298 SOUTHWARK was allocated to Eastbourne and was the first engine Hubert Hobden ever fired on the Cuckoo Line. That 'first firing' involved the 6.10pm Eastbourne-Tunbridge Wells West. PHOTOGRAPH: ANTHONY VENT COLLECTION

The Cuckoo Line on a glorious summer day in 1928 – not bad surroundings in which to earn one's living! We are looking north towards Mayfield – the station can be seen in the distance. PHOTOGRAPH: ANTHONY VENT COLLECTION

We couldn't resist closing with a couple of pictures of the line in later years. This is 28 July 1949, and H class 0-4-4T No.31182 entering Heathfield with the 5.56pm Eastbourne-Tunbridge Wells West. PHOTOGRAPH: S.C.NASH

When working from Eastbourne shed in LB&SCR days, Hubert Hobden could hardly have envisaged something like this on the Cuckoo Line. This is 1950, and a powerful, almost new, LMS-designed (but Brighton-built) Fairburn 2-6-4T emerges from Argos Hill Tunnel with the 11.8am Victoria-Eastbourne. PHOTOGRAPH: S.C.NASH

TRANSPORTER OF DELIGHTS - and

OK – the Widnes Transporter Bridge didn't carry a railway line, nor was it railway-owned. But the transporter car *did* run on rails, so we thought it might just about qualify for inclusion here. That's our argument, m'lud.

Despite its somewhat tenuous 'railway' links, the Widnes Transporter Bridge was a very striking piece of engineering. However, it was not the first bridge across the River Mersey at Widnes – the L&NWR had completed its sturdy 315-yard-long lattice girder bridge between Runcorn and Widnes in 1869. The railway bridge had a footpath, pedestrians being charged one penny to cross. The only alternative to walking over the high, wind-swept gangway was a passenger ferry, but during the first half of the 1890s the ferry services were seriously interrupted by engineering works for the Manchester Ship Canal. The general dissatisfaction with the ferry services, combined with a continuing increase in road transport, soon prompted thoughts of a vehicular crossing.

In 1899 a group of prominent local businessmen formed the Widnes & Runcorn Bridge Company with the object of providing a toll-bearing vehicular crossing. Among the businessmen was Sir John Brunner who later joined forces with Ludwig Mond to establish the well-known alkali works at Winnington. As any river crossing had to leave adequate headroom for shipping to pass underneath, the obvious options were a very high bridge or an opening bridge. But there was a much more practical option – a transporter bridge. The contracts for the construction of the bridge were let in August 1901, that for the superstructure being awarded to Arrols Bridge & Roof Company. After various delays, the bridge was eventually opened on 29 May 1905. The final bill for its construction was £137,663.

The Widnes Transporter Bridge had a span of 1,000 feet supported by pylons 190 feet high which were bedded into solid rock. The transporter car, which was about 12 feet above high water level and which cleared the Ship Canal wall by about 4ft 6in, was driven by electricity which was generated on site. A contemporary account of the structure explained that the transporter car was '...capable of holding at one time four two-horse waggons and 300 passengers. Special accommodation is provided for passengers for protection from the weather by a glazed shelter with folding doors at the end and side. On top of the car is fixed the operator's cabin in which is placed the switchboard so that the operator has a full view of the course and has the car quite at his command. He can thus reverse, go ahead, or put the brake on at a moment's notice. The time occupied by the car is about two and a half minutes; allowing time for loading and unloading it is thus capable of making about nine or ten trips per hour. *(In everyday operation the usual maximum was seven trips per hour.)* The bridge approaches and car are illuminated with electric light, and fog signals and bell which are to be sounded when necessary...'.

Despite being such a grand structure, the bridge's early history was somewhat chequered. The morning after it opened it broke down, and was out of action for nine weeks. Even when it was up and running again it operated at a loss – between 1905 and 1910 it lost an average of £1,000 a year. The outcome was that, in May 1911, Sir John Brunner personally paid off the debts so that the bridge company could *give* the structure to Widnes Corporation. After a couple of successful years the new proprietors gave the bridge a major overhaul which included reducing the weight of the car and installing a new driving system, the electricity for which was now supplied by the Mersey Power Company.

As the years progressed road traffic increased, and by the 1950s the bridge often struggled to meet the demands made upon it. Almost every day there were lengthy queues of cars and lorries on both sides of he river, and if the weather were very windy – and remember that this *is* a somewhat exposed location – the services had to be suspended completely because it was not possible for the car to 'dock'. There were also dangers from the bridge itself – it was far from uncommon for bits of the upper structure to fall off and hit vehicles on the car below, and on one occasion a foot passenger was killed when a chunk of metal from the mechanism almost 100 feet above fell on him. Another oft-heard grumble was that, as the bridge stopped running at 11.30pm, late-shift workers wishing to get home after that time had to use the footway on the railway bridge while motorists and commercial drivers were faced with a 12-mile detour via Warrington.

After prolonged complaints from the public, the construction of a new toll-free road bridge, sandwiched between the old railway bridge and the transporter bridge, was authorised in 1955. At this time the transporter bridge was carrying about 1,000 vehicles and 4,000 foot passengers each day – such a demand would have been beyond its promoters wildest dreams fifty years earlier.

The new road bridge opened to the public at 6pm on 21 July 1961, and this made the transporter bridge immediately obsolete. However, a special 'farewell' crossing for 250 invited guests was made the following morning, 22 July. The car was specially painted silver for the occasion. The demolition of the transporter bridge commenced on 23 July.

Photographs by Douglas Robinson

The transporter bridge, viewed from the Runcorn side in July 1960.

ars and bikes and people and...

Above. A picture taken from the car as it approaches the Widnes side, June 1960.

Left. This view of the Runcorn end of the bridge shows the new road bridge under construction on the left. A fine selection of period vehicles are on view, but we are a little bemused by the 'Low Bridge, 14' 6" Headroom' sign on the side of the road – presumably this referred to the headroom on the transporter car itself.

Right. A closer view of the transporter car leaving Runcorn in July 1960. The notice above the deck states 'Drivers Must Engage Hand-Brake firmly'. Given the proliferation of motor scooters, perhaps the Mod era came to this part of the world rather early.

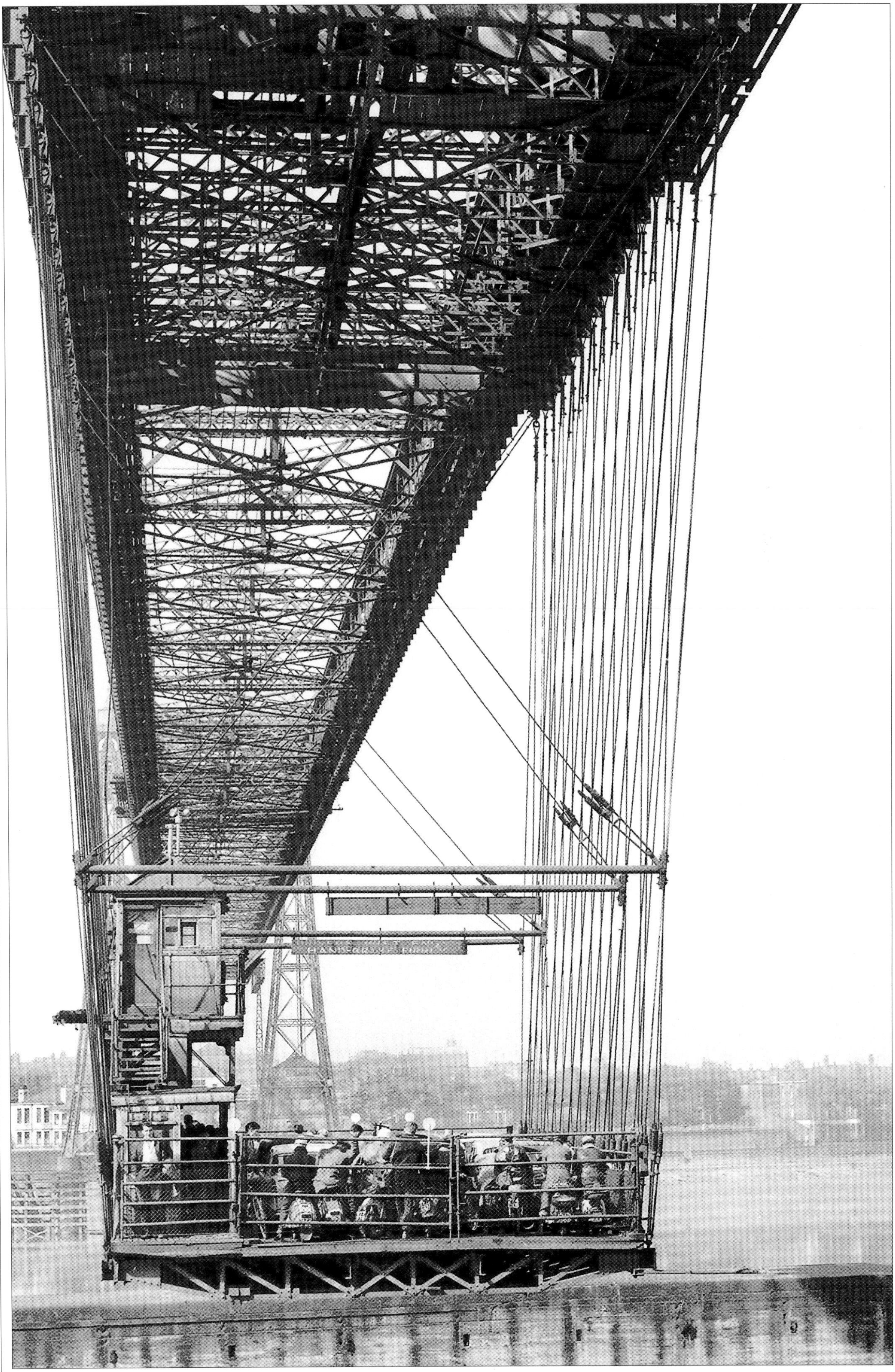

It has been remarked of the old Dublin & South Eastern Railway that it was hard to decide whether it was the largest of the small Irish railways or the smallest of the large railways in that island. Whatever the case, the DSER is remembered mostly as a suburban or 'commuter' line, though its rails stretched far south to Wexford and Waterford, and my schoolfellows, even in the Great Southern era that had begun with the 1925 Grouping, still called it the 'Dirty Slow and Easy'. That was somewhat unfair, as passengers have always brought their dirt with them, but Dubliners were usually ready to knock their railways... The DSER was the line I lived beside for the first eight years of my life, and I knew those initials when I first learned the alphabet.

The portion of the DSER that handled the busy suburban traffic had of course been built by the Dublin & Kingstown, Ireland's first railway company, and opened in December 1834 from its city terminus at Westland Row to the new harbour of Kingstown (since 1921 named Dun Laoghaire – pronounced 'Dun Leary' – as the maps spelt the name of the original fishing village and its miniscule harbour). For the first couple of miles out of Westland Row the railway was carried on an embankment between massive retaining walls before it descended to ground level. The D&K workshops were situated on this high level line at a point where it bridged the Grand Canal Dock. Their situation had come about thus: a disused distillery was situated at the lineside and other local distillers, fearing competition should it be re-activated, subsidised the Kingstown company's purchase of the premises. Here, miracles were performed in cramped circumstances, locomotives and carriages being built 'in house'. The works were taken over by the Dublin Wicklow & Wexford Railway (the old name for the DSER) when it leased the D&K, abandoning its own shops on an even more cramped site in Bray. The works continued to service an increased number of locomotives and rolling stock, but a separate running shed was built on the opposite side of the line, overlooking the canal basin. From here, loco coal was delivered almost to the coaling stage.

Grand Canal Street shed had three roads with room for fifteen locomotives under the cover of a triple-ridged roof which was hipped at the ends. Repairs were carried out on the middle road, at the down end of which was the impressive but old-fashioned shear-legs that features in several of the accompanying photographs. In 1951 it was the practice for outgoing locomotives to progress along the shed road nearest the down line and reverse along the latter (when called) to a trailing crossover opposite the running shed, from where they proceeded to the required platform at Westland Row. This station had grown in importance following the closure of the old Broadstone terminus of the former Midland Great Western Railway in 1937. Trains for Galway and the North-west now departed from Westland Row, where I saw my first Pullman car in 1939. The GSR had three of them.

Studying the photographs taken in the 1950s, I notice that track alterations between 1951 and 1953 caused the removal of the crossover already mentioned. It was repositioned, still between up and down main lines, at the north end of the shed. At about the same time a dead-end siding on the up side was given a facing connection to the up main, in effect making it a goods loop. A loading dock was built alongside this siding. From memory, this was in connection with the conversion of the old Grand Canal Street works (needless to say, it had been closed as quickly as possible by the GSR) into a meat processing plant. This does not seem to have had a long life; apartments for the young, upwardly mobile now occupy the site. On the Dock side of the shed were about three sidings; that next to the shed was a parking lot for engines when space was short, and the remainder gave access to the coal stacks.

The majority of locomotives on the Grand Canal Street roster were tank engines for the suburban services to Dun Laoghaire and Bray, but there was also a handful of tender engines: 4-4-0s for the Wexford and Rosslare passenger workings (a very sparse service in the 1950s) and a few 0-6-0s for goods –these included the fast-dwindling ex-DSE Class J8 engines. One of the two big inside-cylindered moguls was usually to be seen. These, GSR 461 and 462, worked the goods and cattle traffic to and from North Wall across the Liffey and were available for passenger trains when required. They were personal favourites; a very early memory was seeing one standing on the down line at Serpentine Avenue level crossing with one or two officials performing some mystery at ballast level. The black livery with red lining stuck in my mind as did the red D S E R on the tender. The engine must have been on a trial trip after a works visit. The story of their delivery from Beyer Peacock of Manchester in 1922 (as DSER 15 and 16) has been told more than once; with a civil war in the south playing merry hell with the best of DSER engines and carriages, the Beyers were diverted to Belfast and given asylum in Adelaide shed on the Great Northern until it was safe for them to go to Dublin.

The very last engines ordered by the DSER also came from Beyer's. Built in 1924, their works numbers were 6204 and 6205, DSER numbers 34 and 35. They were 4-4-2 tank engines with 6ft drivers and 18in x 26in cylinders, working pressure 175lb and 17,405lb tractive effort at 85% boiler pressure. The Beyer 4-4-2Ts were built with Belpaire fireboxes and the top edges of the side tanks were rounded off in the Scottish fashion also found on Kitson-built engines. The style had been taken up by the Canal Street drawing office and used on their very similar 4-4-2T No.20 which was built by the DSER in 1911 and named KING GEORGE to commemorate the Sovereign's visit to Dublin in that year. No.20 became GSR 455 and, while the name on the engine could not have lasted beyond 1921, the DSER drivers knew it as King George for many years. The GSR classified all three 4-4-2Ts as C2, the Beyers being numbered 456 and 457. All three spent their lives in the Dublin area, though there had been an idea of putting them on main line duties, taking advantage of the big driving wheels. However, 457 was seen outside Limerick works in June 1959.

There were three other DSER bogie tanks, classified C3 by the GSR and built by Sharp Stewart in 1893 to work the through boat trains between Kingsbridge (the Great Southern & Western Railway terminus) and Kingstown Pier via the newly-built Drumcondra line around the north side of Dublin to Amiens Street Junction and the 'Loop Line' to Westland Row. The varied make-up of that train was something to be looked for on summer evenings and triggered my abiding interest in railway carriages. Its most eye-catching item was the Great Northern bogie van with its barred windows and gleaming varnished mahogany finish. The

GRAND CANAL STREET SHED
Words and photographs by Desmond Coakham

Westland Row station, the original city terminus of the Dublin & Kingstown Railway, was described by the locomotive historian E.L.Ahrons as 'a dingy, dirty shed with one platform'. He wrote of what he saw in the 1870s*, but the station had been rebuilt by the end of the 19th century and the train shed still looked respectable when photographed on 12 April 1952. The big mogul, 461, ex-DSER but with a GSR boiler, is seen shunting empty carriages, presumably deputising for the usual station pilot. *(* Ahrons' description of a 'one platform' station is misleading. The station had two platforms, though one was for the exclusive use of the LNWR for its Kingstown-Holyhead traffic.)*

three Sharp Stewart tanks became GSR Nos.458, 459 and 460 and performed the same duties as the C2s. The former had 18in x 26in cylinders and 5ft 3in driving wheels, working at 150lbs. The GSR diagram does not quote tractive effort, but if you have the formula I understand that it can be calculated from the foregoing figures.

The backbone of DSER suburban motive power up to dieselisation were GSR classes F1 and F2, eleven 2-4-2 tank engines that had evolved through rebuilding and renewal from the previous generation of 2-4-0Ts in the capable hands of Richard Cronin, the company's Locomotive Superintendent from 1897 to 1917. Grand Canal Street works are credited with building – or rebuilding – all these engines between 1898 and 1911. A twelfth engine (of class F2, designated GSR 429) was scrapped on acquisition in 1925 along with several assorted casualties from the 'troubles'. Amalgamation came not a moment too soon for the depleted locomotive, carriage and wagon stock of the DSER.

The only basic difference between F1 (Nos.434-439) and F2 (Nos.428-433) was in the coupled wheelbase – 8ft 1in for the F1s and 7ft 10in for the F2s. Other principal dimensions were similar for the two classes: cylinders 17in x 24in, coupled wheels 5ft 6in, boiler pressure 150lb and tractive effort 13,400lb. The boilers of both types were interchangeable with each other, and the GSR changed boilers with impunity. Three F1s had been built with Belpaire boilers and one F2 (No.430) was given a Belpaire boiler by CIE in 1948. This engine had been on loan to the Belfast & Co.Down Railway during World War II, while another of that class (No.432) had been even further away for many years, being withdrawn at Cork in 1957 after branch line work on the erstwhile Cork Bandon & South Coast Railway. I was fortunate in having photographed several of the 2-4-2Ts during the 1950s and many detail variations were not noticed until the results were appraised when these notes were being prepared.

Even smaller and older than the 2-4-2 tanks were the three delightful G1 class

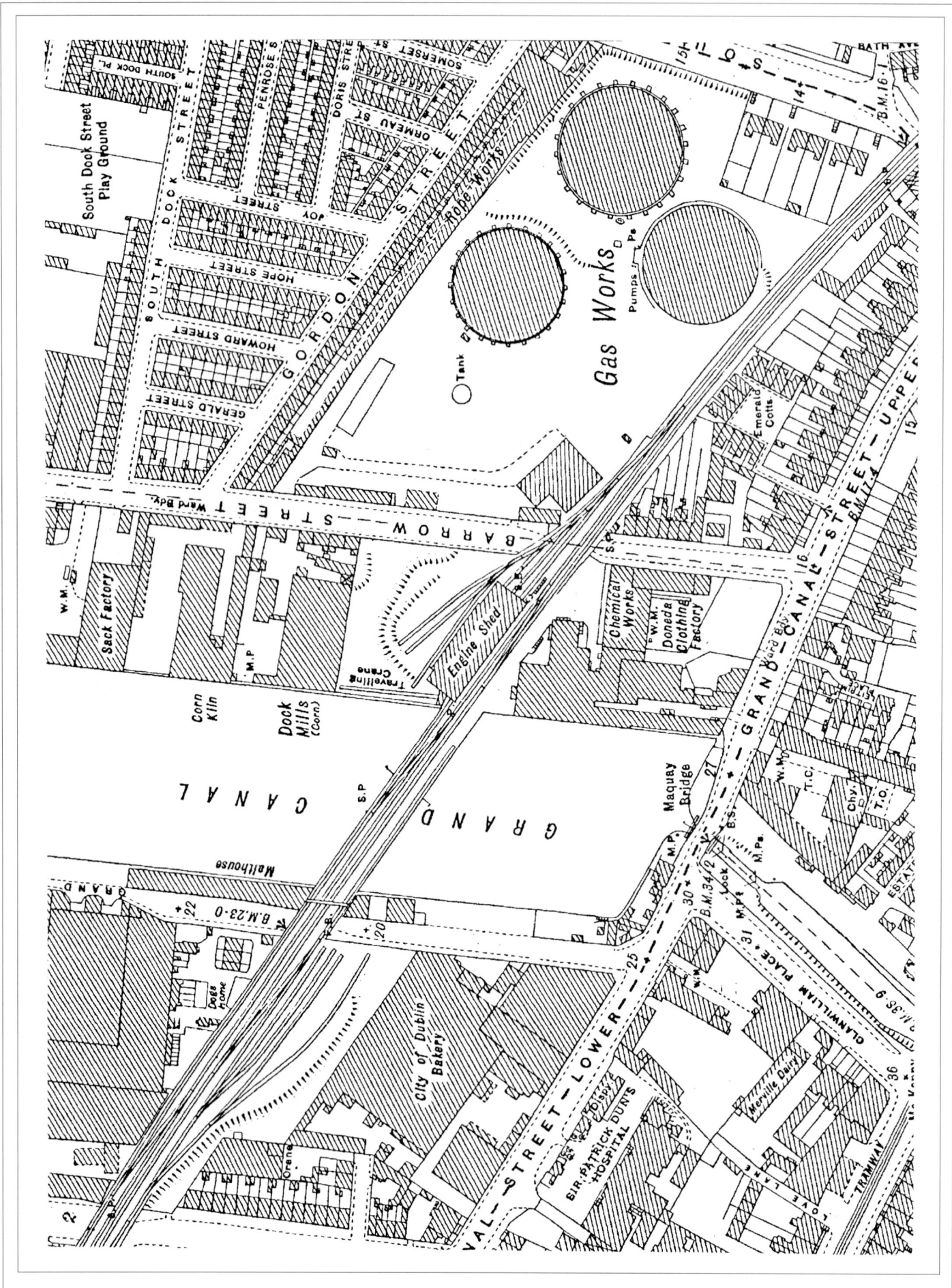

2-4-0 tanks, GSR Nos.423, 424 and 425. The eldest of the trio was 425 (1889); 424 followed in 1890 and 423 in 1891. The last-named was also exiled to Cork at an early date where it was Albert Quay yard shunter until 1955. There was always work for the other two on their home ground in spite of their limited fuel and water capacity. No.425 was given a rather angular bunker extension around 1950 but was withdrawn in 1953; 424 had gone the year before. Their principal dimensions were: cylinders 16in x 24in; coupled wheels 5ft 6in; boiler pressure 140lb. I have written elsewhere (*Railway Bylines Annual No.5*) about the ex-CBSCR 4-6-0T, No.466, that spent several years on Dublin suburban work. However, this engine was never on shed at Grand Canal Street shed during my visits in the 1950s. It was probably a Bray engine. Fifty years of hindsight now suggests that another half an hour's dalliance at the lineside on 4 April 1953

A down local passes Grand Canal Street shed on 11 April 1950. It is hauled by F2 class 2-4-0T No.430, a former DSER which had been fitted with a Belpaire boiler in 1949. On the right is F1 class 439 which has the round top firebox as well as volute bearing springs, fashionable on the DSER in the early 20th century.

might have seen 466 calling at the shed to top up her tanks and that undersized bunker.

Until the success of the Derby-built W class 2-6-4Ts introduced by the LMSR (Northern Counties Committee) in 1947, large tank engines had made little headway in Ireland. The GS&WR 4-8-0T No.900 made its debut in 1915, and a sister, 901, came out nine years later, when their designer (E.A.Watson) had already left Inchicore (the principal works of the GSR and, later, CIE) to become Beyer, Peacock's General Manager. Thus arose one of Ireland's railway mysteries, for they were short-lived but, being banking engines, have no place in the Dublin suburban story. The 'Baltics' of the County Down Railway appeared in 1921 and proved little better than their own predecessors, and by 1925 the GSR drawing office was scheming a large tank engine for the Dublin suburban lines that emerged in 1928 as a 'prairie' tank, the solitary P class No.850. The word 'solitary' says it all. The leading dimensions of this 2-6-2T were: cylinders (outside) 17½in x 28in, coupled wheels 5ft 6in, working pressure 160lb, tractive effort 17,700lb, water capacity 1,700 gallons, coal capacity 3 tons, weight in working order 71 tons 10 cwt, maximum axle load 16 tons. This massive looking engine was no great improvement on existing DSE section motive power, even with a superheater. When Inchicore Works turned out more locomotives for Dublin suburban services in 1933, the 0-6-2 arrangement was chosen for the five engines, Nos.670-674. Classified I3, they had inside cylinders of 18in x 24in and coupled wheels of 5ft 6in. There were modern-looking (for the time) chimneys, wide diameter, but their domes appeared somewhat undersized. They were the only GSR locomotives not to carry cast numberplates; instead, they had large numerals painted in yellow on the side tanks. CIE made this standard practice. We did not have train-timers who logged the speed of 'all-stations' trains, but the 670s seemed to carry out their duties without fuss. They also were superheated.

By the mid-fifties the writing was on the wall; diesel power was arriving in quantity and Grand Canal Street shed was required for the Metro-Vick locomotives which were taking over the long-distance services. The dwindling band of 'suburban tanks' migrated across town to the former Midland Great Western running shed at the Broadstone, taking with them their venerable breakdown van. The last withdrawal dates for the classes we have reviewed are as follows: C2 – 1959, C3 – 1960, F1 – 1952, F2 – 1957, G1 – 1955, I3 – 1960, P1 – 1955.

I began this article by questioning the DSER's position in the pecking order of Irish railways, and I believe I have answered the question by what has been written. Let us say it was the 'smallest of the larger companies' for one important reason: its Locomotive Superintendent had a drawing office under his command. Its last two bogie tanks, taken into stock in 1924, were tendered for by Beyer, Peacock & Co to the drawings and specifications issued by George Wild, the DSER's locomotive engineer. In that same year two other 4-4-2 tank engines, rather larger than the DSER examples, were being completed in the same erecting shop at Gorton Works to the makers' drawings. They were for one of the smaller Irish companies – the Belfast & Co.Down – and only one 'progressive number', to use Beyer's own phrase, separated the BCDR pair (W/Nos.6201/6202) and the DSER pair (6204/6205). The BCDR locomotive engineer had one salaried assistant and no drawing office. Its trains ran over a smaller route mileage but handled a denser volume of traffic and it paid a respectable dividend on its shares (though this would cease very soon). If both companies had ordered the Beyer design they would each have saved money and the DSER would have acquired engines every bit as good as the ones they got. But the enthusiasts would not have had as much pleasure…

My best thanks to Peter Rowledge, who provided a most useful set of GSR engine diagrams and much food for thought, and to Messrs. Shepherd and Beesley for their DSER book, again a most useful work of reference.

DUBLIN

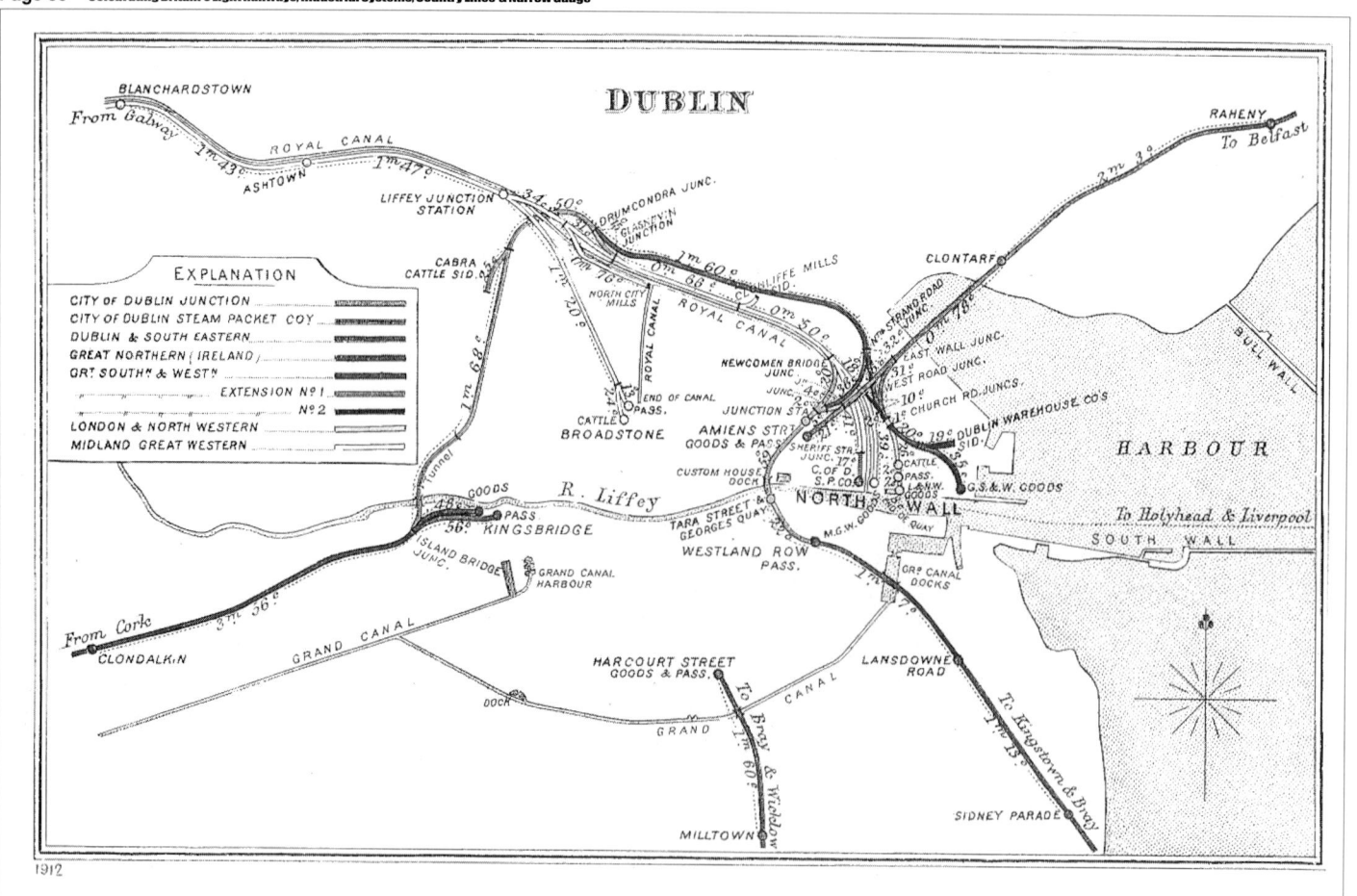

EXPLANATION
CITY OF DUBLIN JUNCTION
CITY OF DUBLIN STEAM PACKET COY
DUBLIN & SOUTH EASTERN
GREAT NORTHERN (IRELAND)
GR? SOUTH? & WEST?
              EXTENSION N? 1
                        N? 2
LONDON & NORTH WESTERN
MIDLAND GREAT WESTERN

1912

One of the later examples of the DSER's F1 class 2-4-2Ts, No.438, passes Grand Canal Street shed on 2 June 1951. The engine and train are less well turned out than in the previous picture. This engine had been built in 1906 with a Belpaire boiler and round-top side tanks, but by the time this picture was taken it had lost the former. There was a difference in boiler pitch: 7ft 7in for the F1s and 7ft 3in for the F2s, reflected in chimney and dome sizes. Standardisation was difficult to achieve at Inchicore Works.

An up train this time, headed by the ex-CB&SCR 4-6-0T No.466 on 4 April 1953. The gasholders in the background belong to the Alliance and Dublin Consumers' Gas Company and have long since been replaced by natural gas. The new up loop is in the foreground.

Only a few ex-DSER goods engines remained to be taken into CIE stock in 1945, and they did not stray far from their home ground. Here is 443 on shed, with a glimpse of Dublin dockland behind. This 0-6-0 was one of two built by the DSER in 1904/5 with 5ft 1in wheels. They were lumped together with three others by the GSR as J8, in spite of varying cylinder dimensions and boiler pressures.

Another J8, No.444, stands in front of the shear-legs on 4 April 1953, newly painted in 'genuine' black (not the old dark grey). Built at Canal Street in 1910, this one had 4ft 11½in wheels, 18½in x 26in cylinders and a different style cab.

A regular sight at Canal Street was 455 (the erstwhile KING GEORGE), though this picture was taken at Bray on a wet April day in 1952. It is included to show the locomotive's final condition, not long after receiving a Belpaire boiler in place of the round-top previously carried. The drivers liked the old 'King' and one wonders whether the new boiler made any difference to its performance. It carried the CIE green livery in its last years.

Also included in the GSR's C2 class were the two almost modern bogie tanks built by Beyer Peacock in 1924, the last year of the DSER's separate existence. Note that 456 had rounded top edges to the side tanks (like 455 and 457), a Kitson trademark, and bore no obvious Beyer features. They had been designed in the DSER drawing office. 456 is shown in CIE green at Grand Canal Street on 4 April 1953.

No.458 – one of the earlier (C3) 4-4-2 tanks by Sharp Stewart – leaves Grand Canal Street shed on 2 June 1951.

The last of the Sharp Stewart trio, 460, rests outside Grand Canal Street shed on 2 June 1951. Neither 460 nor 458 (seen in the previous picture) received CIE green livery – the only one of the C3s to receive that livery was 459.

F2 class 2-4-2T No.433 was station pilot at Westland Row on 11 April 1950 and also carried the green livery.

The smallest of DSER survivors were the three G1 class 2-4-0 tank engines. This is 424 on 28th March 1951.

Another picture taken on 28 March 1951 – this time we see G1 No.425 standing near the coal sidings. Behind it is a mobile steam crane with its jib down.

A rear view of 425 taken in 1950 showing how Inchicore enlarged the bunker in a somewhat brutal manner.

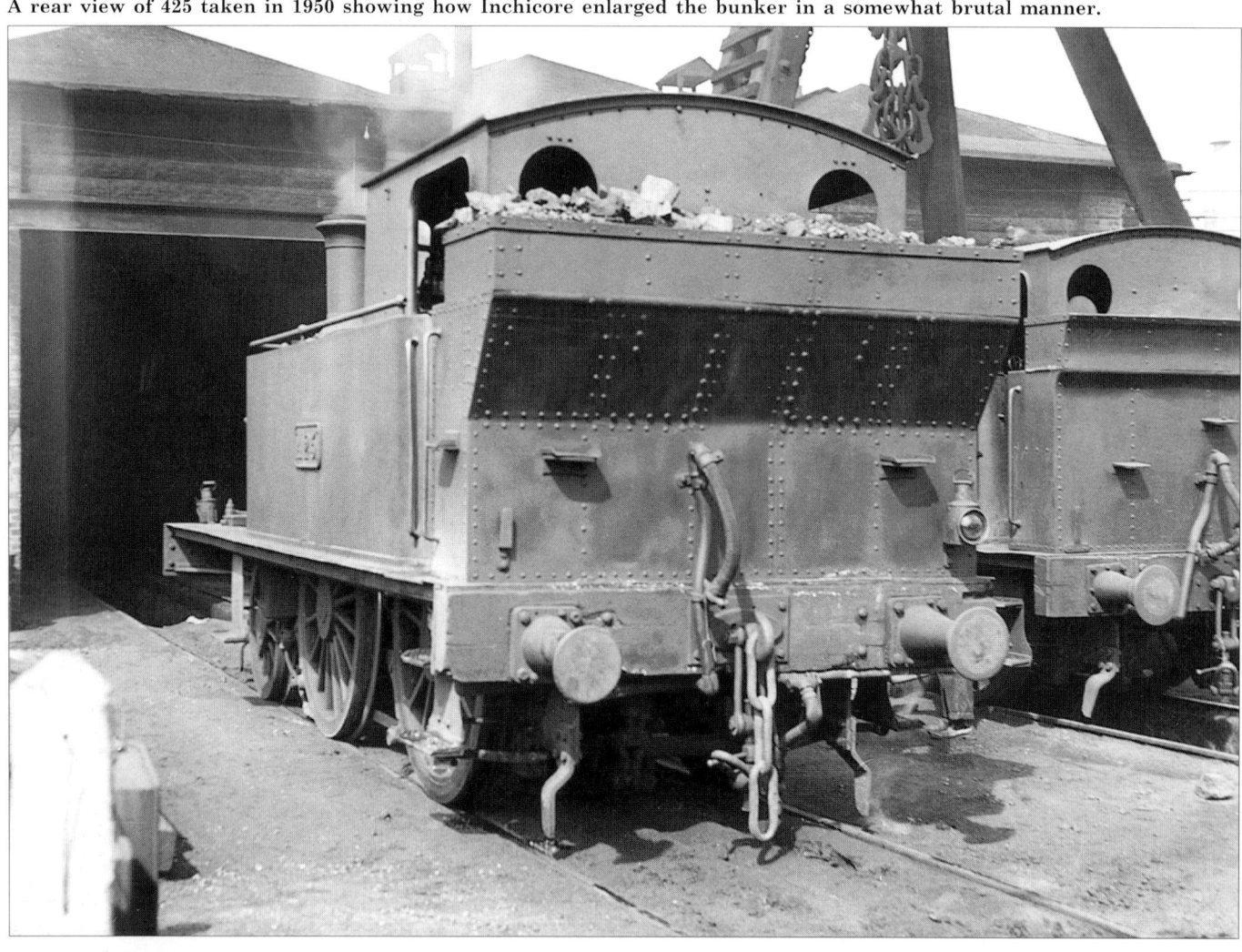

The solitary P1 2-6-2T No.850 is arrayed in CIE green livery, as befits the largest suburban tank engine on the system. The date is 28 March 1951.

One of the I3 class suburban 0-6-2Ts, No.673, was on shed at Canal Street on 2 June 1951. It had lost its original chimney and dome and the replacements of a more traditional pattern did not suit it as well.

A Lion and a Bear in lieu of cats with no tails
Photographs by Douglas Robinson

And finally...

The 2ft gauge Groudle Glen Railway on the Isle of Man opened in 1896 and closed for good in 1962. Throughout its life it had had only two locomotives, a pair of almost identical Bagnall 2-4-0Ts named SEA LION and POLAR BEAR. (We *knew* you were going to ask... Sorry, but we haven't a clue why the locomotives were named after creatures which are not exactly native to the Isle of Man.) Our two pictures were both taken at The Headland. The upper picture shows SEA LION taking water in July 1957 and our lower picture shows the redundant POLAR BEAR in July 1962 – i.e. after the railway had closed. Both engines were later saved for preservation: SEA LION went to the Steam Centre at Kirk Michael on the Isle of Man while POLAR BEAR went to Brockham Museum in Surrey.